MAGNUS SKJÖLD

City State

Reykjavík in Context

First published by Mjaldur Publishing 2024

Copyright © 2024 by Magnus Skjöld

All rights reserved. No part of this publication may be reproduced, stored or transmitted in any form or by any means, electronic, mechanical, photocopying, recording, scanning, or otherwise without written permission from the publisher. It is illegal to copy this book, post it to a website, or distribute it by any other means without permission.

Magnus Skjöld asserts the moral right to be identified as the author of this work.

Magnus Skjöld has no responsibility for the persistence or accuracy of URLs for external or third-party Internet Websites referred to in this publication and does not guarantee that any content on such Websites is, or will remain, accurate or appropriate.

Designations used by companies to distinguish their products are often claimed as trademarks. All brand names and product names used in this book and on its cover are trade names, service marks, trademarks and registered trademarks of their respective owners. The publishers and the book are not associated with any product or vendor mentioned in this book. None of the companies referenced within the book have endorsed the book.

First edition

ISBN: 9798872216261

Cover art by Irene Giua

This book was professionally typeset on Reedsy. Find out more at reedsy.com

To Heiða

Contents

Preface iii
Acknowledgement xi

I Cities and Urbanisation

1. The Triumph of the Cities 3
2. What is a City? 10
3. Does Size Matter? 15
4. Reykjavík in Comparison with Similar Cities 20

II Environment, History, and Planning

5. Nature and Climate 37
6. A Danish Outpost 44
7. The Birth of a Capital 54
8. Concrete and Parking Spots 59

III Reykjavík Politics

9. The Town by the Blue Channels 69
10. The Long Reign of the Independence Party 77
11. The City Flourishes 80
12. The Reykjavík List 85
13. The Chaos 90

| 14 | The Best Party | 94 |
| 15 | The New Urbanites | 97 |

IV The People

16	The Reykjavíkians and Their Neighbours	105
17	Immigration	117
18	Double Residency	122
19	A Promised Land	128
20	Destination Reykjavík	135
21	A Clash of Cultures	146
22	Nationalism, the Nordic Countries and Europe	153
23	The European Trajectory	161

V The Future

| 24 | Reykjavík and International Politics | 169 |
| 25 | The Lessons from Living in Harsh and Remote Areas | 173 |

Epilogue	179
Notes	182
About the Author	195
Also by Magnus Skjöld	197

Preface

The significance of Reykjavík within Icelandic society is overwhelming in every aspect. Numerous works have explored the city's history and its role in the Icelandic community. This book delves into these subjects to some extent, examining the politics, economy, and culture of the Icelandic people in the context of the capital city and its potential future as a driving force and framework for life in the North Atlantic. It prompts us to ponder whether there are lessons to be learned from the city's journey—lessons that can benefit us all in the uncertain future we have shaped through our actions since the Industrial Revolution.

Iceland is a country of contrasts. From being the poorest country in Europe at the beginning of the 20th century, it has transformed into one of the wealthiest. The Icelandic economy's booms and busts are more pronounced than in other developed economies. Following the remarkable rise of the Icelandic financial system in the early 2000s, it experienced one of the most significant bankruptcies in the history of finance, not per capita, but in real terms. In the 2010s, the Icelandic tourism industry experienced rapid growth, with the number of tourists increasing from around half a million per year to over two million in a decade. However, the COVID-19 pandemic brought the tourism industry to a standstill. Now, tourists have returned in even greater numbers than before. This is the reality of life on this island in the North Atlantic. Everything is slightly more extreme compared to neighbouring countries.

This book focuses on Reykjavík and its importance to the Icelandic people, who inhabit this northern island known as the "Land of the Midnight Sun" or " of Fire and Ice" (take your pick). It also explores the city's climate, history, and changes in recent decades. Reykjavík has been a destination for immigration, both from within the country and abroad, with foreign citizens accounting for 18.1% of the population in 2023.[1]

Cities play a crucial role in shaping every era of human existence. Their growth and development, architecture, demographics, production, languages, and sources of inspiration are all vital factors. Cities are the imprints of culture, from which we embark into the future while reflecting on the past. Human history has predominantly unfolded within cities, starting from the earliest settlements in Mesopotamia and the Middle East around 4500 BC, such as Uruk, Eridu, Byblos, Jericho, Aleppo, and Jerusalem. Later came the Greek city-states, Athens, Sparta, and Mycenaean Troy. Then Rome, the numerous cities in India and China, the commercial hubs of the Middle Ages like Venice, Genoa, and the Hanseatic League, the industrial cities of the modern age such as Manchester and Birmingham, and the "megacities" of the 21st century like Tokyo, Shanghai, New York, and Mumbai. Within these cities, the pulse of humanity beats at any given time.

Reykjavík is typically recognised as the sole city on the island of Iceland. It was mainly built in the twentieth century, evident in its planning and architecture. However, remnants of the more distant past and the nation's history can still be found both within the city itself and its immediate surroundings. For the longest time, the ruling powers in Iceland, or their local representatives, have resided in the area we now refer to as the capital region, that is Reykjavík, along with the surrounding municipalities.

Reykjavík is a small city. The Reykjavík municipality's total population is 140,000 inhabitants, which is relatively small on an international scale. However, the Reykjavík area is more densely populated, with approximately 245,000 people in the metropolitan region, making it the fourteenth largest urban region in the Nordic countries in terms of population. Consequently, the Reykjavík area is gradually approaching the population size that typically accommodates infrastructure like light rail systems, common to many cities of comparable size in the Nordic countries and northern Europe. Plans for such developments are already underway and moving closer to implementation. Reykjavík's economic influence extends even further, reaching places like Selfoss to the east, Reykjanesbær to the south, and Borgarnes to the north. People residing in these areas commute to work in the city on a daily basis.

Reykjavík has been described as one of the most isolated cities in the world. The nearest city of comparable size, Aberdeen in Scotland, is over 1,300 km away in a straight line, south to the British Isles. To find another city of similar size, Bergen in Norway, with around 256,000 inhabitants, one must fly approximately 1,500 km southeast over the North Sea. It has been suggested that the city is "completely alone" in this regard, lacking neighbouring cities to draw inspiration from.[2] However, Reykjavík is not truly isolated. Transportation between Reykjavík and other cities has always been relatively accessible, by sea or by air, at least since the city started to take shape.

In Iceland, there are differing views on the role of Reykjavík, which can be broadly classified into two perspectives. On one hand, some want the city to be a service centre for people who may not necessarily reside within its metropolitan area. From this viewpoint, Reykjavík serves as a hub where all Icelanders can seek healthcare, entertainment and interact with the public sector. On the other hand, some place greater emphasis on catering to the needs of the city's residents. They want Reykjavík to be a vibrant, densely populated, and well-organized place that attracts talented individuals, even from abroad. Despite the often inclement weather and the palpable darkness during the midwinter months, they consider Reykjavík an excellent place to live, raise children, work, play, and flourish.

Most people's perspectives fall somewhere in between, and can even fluctuate by the prevailing weather conditions. It is easier to believe in cycling to work or relying on the imperfect public transportation system when the storm abates and the sun graces the calm, clear air of this northernmost capital city in the world. However, when a storm strikes, drenching everyone even through the sturdiest protective garments, it becomes more tempting to seek refuge in the nearest car and navigate the streets between buildings. There is also the perpetual challenge of finding parking in proximity to one's errands at any given time.

These varying viewpoints, addressed within the Reykjavík City Council, municipal councils of neighbouring towns, the national parliament Alþingi, and the government and administrative systems at both the city and national levels, reflect the norm. Reykjavík holds significant importance in Icelandic life, hosting a large portion of the country's economic, cultural, and political activities. It serves as the country's gateway and represents it economically and culturally.

This significance also shapes the image that the city wishes to project. Reykjavík proudly holds the title of "City of Literature" and is included on UNESCO's list of such cities. The UNESCO listing is dedicated to the preservation, dissemination, and education surrounding Icelandic sagas and medieval literary works, as well as various literary projects.[3] Reykjavík also strives to present itself as an environmentally friendly city—a stronghold of sustainability—and has received international recognition for its efforts.[4] Each house in the city is heated geothermally using hot water from the depths of the Earth, and electricity is generated by hydroelectric power plants, though the environmental friendliness of such plants remains a topic of debate. However, Reykjavík is also a city where 75% to 85% of all trips within the capital area are made by car,[5] placing it among the highest in the world for intra-city travel by private vehicles.

Reykjavík has been called the "Shangri-La of the North",[6] referring to the high life expectancy of the inhabitants, the abundance of excellent restaurants, relatively low pollution, proximity to nature, and the hot springs used for heating houses. These hot springs also form the basis for the magnificent swimming pools throughout the capital and country. Reykjavík is a positive and cosy city on the edge of the inhabited world. However, it has also acquired the role of the villain. During the dark autumn days of 2008, when the world's financial system collapsed, the city of London earned the nickname "Reykjavík on the Thames" in the British media due to the fallen Icelandic banks, which had flown too close to the sun like ancient Icarus, melting their wings and falling to the ground. Nevertheless, notoriety can sometimes be preferable to obscurity, and this unwelcome spotlight on the country, the city, and the nation played a role in what followed. Tourists flocked to this mysterious northern land, which had suddenly become relatively affordable to visit due to the collapse of its currency alongside the inflated banks.

In recent years, Reykjavík has undergone significant changes, largely driven by the exponential growth of the tourism industry. The number of tourists visiting the country has grown from about 300 thousand per year around the turn of the century to approximately 2 million in 2019.[7] This represents a more than sixfold increase in tourist arrivals over a span of 20 years, although the COVID-19 pandemic temporarily altered this condition.

Reykjavík serves as a gateway for most tourists exploring the country, and if these visitors were evenly distributed throughout the year, it would mean that there would be approximately 100 thousand people in the country at any given time, exceeding the local population. Therefore, the presence of tourists is akin to a force majeure due to the impact they have on society.

The effects of the tourist boom have been most keenly felt in Reykjavík's old town. Shops in the city centre, sometimes derogatorily referred to as "puffin shops," predominantly sell souvenirs and other goods specifically designed to appeal to and capture the money of foreign tourists. Additionally, the increase in the number of restaurants and cafés caters to tourists seeking refreshments between excursions to the highlands in jeeps, bus trips around the "Golden Circle," or visits to the Blue Lagoon. The influx of tourists has also created a demand for accommodation, with the number of hotel rooms in the city growing from 2,750 in 2010 to around 5,500 in

2023.[8] However, this still falls short of meeting the demand during peak periods, leading to a substantial increase in the availability of "unconventional" accommodations facilitated by the sharing economy, such as homes and apartments in the city centre offered through websites like Airbnb.com.

The rise in tourist numbers has profoundly impacted the appearance and reputation of Reykjavík. The city's festivals and events have also attracted foreign participants. Events like the August Gay Pride, Reykjavík Marathon (also held in August in conjunction with Culture Night), The Midnight Run in June, Reykjavík International Film Festival in September, Reykjavik International Literary Festival held every other year in September, Iceland Airwaves in November, Reykjavík Arts Festival in the spring, and the exuberant New Year's celebrations, complete with extensive fireworks, draw guests and participants from abroad. Consequently, the city's visibility in foreign media and its inclusion on various lists of exciting destinations, both official and unofficial, have increased.

During the summer, Reykjavík transforms into a green city. It could be considered the "largest forest in the country" since no other area in Iceland boasts such a vast number of trees, shrubs, flowers, and green spaces. In certain parts of the city, especially during the bright summer months, the vegetation is so dense that the houses are barely visible. This greenery has improved the liveability of the city, as vegetation reduces wind, creating more sheltered and pleasant areas than the forecasts of the Icelandic Meteorological Office would suggest. The behaviour of Icelanders in the sun reflects their northern nature. While people in warmer countries seek shade, where the temperature might be a comfortable 20-30 degrees Celsius, to escape the sun's rays, Icelanders - under conditions of 12 degrees Celsius in the shade, sit in the sun, where the temperature may be similar, or around 25 degrees Celsius, creating a pleasant outdoor environment. Therefore, the meteorological forecast does not accurately represent the weather in Reykjavík. For Icelanders, 12 degrees Celsius and sunshine are considered good weather, while many individuals from warmer countries might shudder at the thought. Foreign tourists often ask, "What is the average temperature in Iceland during the summer?" The Icelander answers, "About 12 degrees," prompting the foreigner to conclude that the country is an inhospitable, desolate place on the edge of the Arctic— "Iceland."

However, those who reside there know that this is not the case. Despite cursing the wind and horizontal rain out loud, there is something about this country. The crisp arctic air makes the colours more vibrant. The air is fresher. The diversity of nature is immense. And Reykjavík itself is becoming increasingly pleasant, evolving into a mature, medium-sized European city. While there is still much work to be done to strengthen its infrastructure, it compares favourably with other similar cities, as detailed in this book.

These changes have inevitably influenced the identity of the city's residents and administrators, propelling Reykjavík beyond its traditional role of providing local services to the population and tackling significant issues such as human rights, justice, and equality. The city has even ventured into the quagmire of Middle Eastern conflicts, marking a new era for its government as it takes hesitant steps in becoming a "world city" of sorts. Reykjavík aspires to have a voice on the international stage and be a responsible member of the global community. It is the "City State" of Reykjavík.

Acknowledgement

The original edition of this book, titled "Borgríkið: Reykjavík sem framtíð þjóðar," was published in Icelandic in 2020 by Bifröst University. However, the majority of the work was carried out by my friend and publisher, Jónas Sigurgeirsson, through his publishing company Bókafélagið, for which I am deeply grateful. I would also like to express my gratitude to Vilhjálmur Egilsson, the former rector of Bifröst University, for his encouragement and support, without which this book would never have come to fruition.

For this English version, with the help of my colleague Danielle Beauchemin, I have made revisions to account for the fact that it is being published a few years later than the original edition, and certain specific Icelandic nuances have been omitted. I want to extend my thanks to Danielle for her help. Nonetheless, I sincerely hope those who wish to acquaint themselves with the captivating city of Reykjavík will find both inspiration and valuable information within these pages.

Reykjavík, January 2024
  Magnus Skjöld

I

Cities and Urbanisation

1

The Triumph of the Cities

The twentieth century was unquestionably the century of nation-states. Since their emergence in the eighteenth and nineteenth centuries, nation-states have served as the administrative units and international actors around which humanity has rallied. They inherited that role from "empires" that were typically "multinational," characterised by diverse cultures and languages, usually led by a small elite in a dominant state. Influenced by the prevailing ideology of nationalism in the nineteenth century, new borders were established, resulting in mass migrations to create "pure nations" within these borders. Simultaneously, the old empires disintegrated. Austria, a powerful empire in Europe for centuries and a leading force in the Catholic part of the continent for five hundred years is now a small country with an oversized capital. It accommodates government buildings and infrastructure that once belonged to a multinational empire that has since vanished and is unlikely to re-emerge.

"Cities are where history happens" - The Chicago Skyline - Photo by the author

However, nation-states have come under mounting pressure both "from above" – from federations, international organisations like the European Union, and the challenges of globalisation such as the environment, crime, and terrorism, which they cannot address in isolation – and "from below," from regions with their distinct identities like Catalonia and the Basque Country in Spain, Flanders and Wallonia in Belgium, and Scotland in the United Kingdom. Cities have also played a significant role in exerting pressure. In many cases, cities have become like states within states, with substantial administrations possessing resources and responsibilities akin to those of entire countries. Cities such as New York in the United States,

Paris in France, London in the United Kingdom, Istanbul in Turkey, Moscow in Russia, Tel Aviv in Israel, Nairobi in Kenya, Mumbai in India, Shanghai in China, Tokyo in Japan, and Rio de Janeiro in Brazil, among others, attract people regardless of language and culture. Individuals can identify with their city, support local football teams, and lead lives without cultural barriers, even if they do not speak the dominant language of the state or possess its passport.

This characteristic of cities, their magic, and their dynamism have led some to believe that cities are well-suited to assume the roles traditionally held by nation-states in an increasingly globalized and multicultural world. Cities are where history happens, where the majority of humanity resides. In the "global south," formerly known as the Third World, cities have experienced remarkable growth, giving rise to numerous megacities such as Dhaka in Bangladesh, Guangzhou-Foshan (formerly Canton) in China, and Lagos in Nigeria. These developing countries' megacities face significant challenges that far surpass those encountered in the North (or West) on a daily basis. However, they have also been at the forefront of finding innovative solutions, with the human mind pushed to its limits in the slums where survival requires extraordinary efforts.

Before the era of nation-states, city-states existed. The Roman Empire was referred to as the "empire of one city," and ancient Greece had renowned city-states like Athens, Sparta, and Troy. Venice and the northern Italian trading cities of Florence, Bologna, and Genoa were examples of city-states, as were the cities of the Hanseatic League in northern Germany and its surrounding areas. These cities were highly active in trade and commerce in the Baltic Sea and the North Sea from the fifteenth century until the rise of nation-states in the nineteenth century led to the dissolution of the alliance. Cities like Lübeck, Hamburg, and Lüneburg enjoyed considerable autonomy and answered to no ruler other than the Holy Roman Emperor.

If we examine human history, cities have a much longer and more illustrious history as administrative units than states or countries, which are relatively recent phenomena. While nation-states played a vital role in a specific social development and their contributions to the creation, planning, and operation of the welfare state should not be underestimated, it is worth questioning whether they have solidified in their present form.

Author Yuval Noah Harari, in his book "Sapiens," suggests that modern humans essentially live in one "empire"[9] This echoes ideas previously put forth by Michael Hardt and Antonio Negri in their book "Empire"[10]. This concept refers to the international institutional and legal framework that has taken shape since World War II, as well as the underlying norms and principles such as human rights, democracy, and capitalism. This is where conflicts between cities and nation-states can arise, as nation-states often defend nationalistic ideas of the past against the interests of cities that thrive on openness and diverse perspectives.

The Brexit vote in June 2016, where the British people decided to leave the European Union after more than forty years of membership, highlighted a clear contrast between the attitudes of Londoners and those living outside the metropolitan area. Considering the changes occurring within nation-states and the problems their existence creates, it is not surprising that Londoners, who strongly recognised the significance of EU membership for their city, explored the idea of London breaking away from the UK and becoming an independent city-state.[11] Although it may initially seem strange, such a proposition aligns with historical precedent, such as the Holy Roman Empire, which operated similarly. The European Union establishes fundamental rules of conduct in northern Europe, requiring some level of compliance, but cities maintain their independence in various aspects, pursuing trade and communication without being hindered by rural demands and interests.

Despite the vast inequality found within major cities worldwide, they remain a powerful common denominator among their inhabitants. Often, city dwellers who may have little in common are those who lack deep roots in the majority nation and may not even hold citizenship in the country where the city is located. Immigrants often comprise a significant percentage of the population, with approximately one-third of Los Angeles residents and one-quarter of San Francisco residents born outside the United States.[12] Yet, they walk the same streets, attend the same schools, support local sports teams fervently, interact with individuals from diverse backgrounds, and contribute to the city's sense of community. In this regard, cities present a significant challenge to nation-states that were shaped in the nineteenth and twentieth centuries, often with considerable effort. Cities are increasingly intertwined with people's identities and are vying for recognition alongside the nation and nation-state.

These milestones have been punctuated by the fact that urban dwellers now comprise the majority of the global population. This is not surprising, as cities offer enjoyment and a sense of fellowship with others. The competition, relationships, and abundant human resources found in cities foster new ideas and drive economic, cultural, and political progress. Revolutions do usually not arise in rural areas but in urban squares, where people come together to think big and foster innovative thinking.

American political scientist Benjamin R. Barber aimed to leverage the qualities of cities to revolutionise global democracy. His proposal involved connecting cities through what he called the Global Parliament of Mayors. This platform would enable cities to collaborate on addressing pressing challenges like sustainability, cultural diversity, and social justice. Cities, with their ongoing projects and experiences, could contribute to shaping global responses. It is important to note that this initiative would not seek to establish a world government but rather provide a platform for elected representatives from cities around the world—the majority of humanity and 80% of the population in the "developed" world—to exchange ideas and share "best practices." Additionally, the collective purchasing power of cities could be harnessed to elevate the quality of services provided to citizens worldwide.[13]

Barber's idea gained momentum after its introduction in his 2013 book, "If Mayors Ruled the World." The inaugural meeting of the World Congress of Mayors took place in The Hague, Netherlands, in September 2016, with the participation of 75 cities. It is anticipated that numerous cities, both small and large, will join the organisation in the future.[14] The initial agenda of the congress focused on challenges related to refugees and migration, global warming, and administrative matters. Barber worked on a draft parliamentary resolution and a register of citizens' rights, which included innovative proposals such as special IDs or passports granting access to schools, transportation, and welfare services provided by cities. It also addressed the right to take action on issues such as global warming, pollution, and other neglected problems. The resolution emphasised the importance of cross-border collaboration without government interference.[15]

Barber, who passed away on April 24, 2017, shortly after the inaugural meeting, expressed his belief that the International Mayors' Congress could become a significant forum and an alternative to the limited and rhetoric-driven approach of nations in international affairs.[16]

Jane Jacobs, a sociologist from the same country as Barber, made an observation regarding nation-states in the late 20th century. She highlighted that although nation-states possess political and military attributes, they should not be regarded as economic entities, as economic ideas rooted in mercantilism tend to suggest. Assumptions such as GDP and the notion of nations as economic wholes are flawed. When examining countries without bias, it becomes evident that they are composed of diverse economies, encompassing both affluent and impoverished regions within the same nation. Similarly, it is clear that cities play a unique role in shaping and revitalising the economic environment of not only their immediate surroundings but also more distant areas.[17]

2

What is a City?

What is a city? Can Akureyri, the largest urban area in Iceland outside Reykjavík, with around 20,000 inhabitants, be considered a city? Is Tórshavn in the Faroe Islands, which is of a similar size to Akureyri, considered a city? Tórshavn is also the capital of the Faroe Islands. Does it matter? Is population the defining factor for cities, or is there something else? In Iceland, there is an agreement that only Reykjavík, as a municipality, can be called a city, at least officially. The Kópavogur town council proposed in 2011 that the town, which currently has almost 40,000 residents, change its designation from town to city, but the proposal failed to pass.[18] One could argue that a more natural question would be whether the city designation should apply to the entire capital area rather than individual municipalities within it. A subsequent question is whether it would have been more appropriate for the Akureyri area to be designated as a city, despite its municipality being smaller than that of Kópavogur. In fact, this debate has already begun.[19]

Benjamin Barber sought to define cities based on what they

are not. According to him, cities are the opposite of rural, uninhabited places that are visited but not inhabited. The rural represents, sometimes intentionally, the absence of human society, or, as Barber puts it, the idea of Eden before the creation of man and woman.[20] Rural communities are sparsely populated and scattered, but they are also what Barber calls "thick" in terms of their close-knit and well-founded nature, referred to as "Gemeinschaft" in the German philosopher Ferdinand Tönnies' vocabulary. On the other hand, urban communities are "thin" but densely populated and interconnected, referred to as "Gesellschaft" by Tönnies. While rural towns are often isolated, with residents preferring to stay within their homes as much as possible, cities are naturally interconnected and characterised by mobility. As the countryside is primarily based on agriculture, subsistence, and the utilisation of natural resources, cities depend on trade, commerce, and the unhindered flow of goods from everywhere. The city relies on the food production of the countryside, but the countryside does not need the city except as a market for its products.[21]

Moreover, cities serve as workplaces and business centres. This places cities at the heart of the capitalist economy and the information and service economy, which inhibits their role as mere places of subsistence living. Despite the belief that technology would diminish the importance of physical gathering for certain tasks, the opposite has occurred with the information technology revolution. There is no evidence that information technology has reduced the appeal of cities in terms of culture, creativity, communication, and civil society. On the contrary, cities are growing at an unprecedented rate, attracting people in similar sectors to gather in the same places within cities. [22]

All of the above factors characterise the capital area in Iceland, and it is worth discussing to what extent these apply to other urban areas in the country, especially the Akureyri area. Akureyri largely fulfils the conditions required to be considered a city in the traditional and general sense, albeit a very small city.

The proportion of the population living in cities is closely related to a country's economic situation. High-income countries are more likely to have a higher proportion of urban dwellers, while low-income countries tend to have a higher proportion of rural residents. Economists have studied the relationship between urbanisation and economic growth and whether urbanisation leads to economic growth or vice versa. The answer lies somewhere in between. The success of urban businesses attracts people, which in turn leads to further growth.[23] The World Bank has calculated that it is beneficial to locate companies in urban areas. For example, by relocating a factory from a settlement with 1,000 workers to one with 10,000 workers, production increases by 15%.[24] This can be attributed to economies of scale, as people within the same sector can monitor and learn from each other, outsource projects, and take advantage of specialised services. Furthermore, transport and various service costs are reduced due to economies of scale.

However, if it is so economical to have people in cities, wouldn't it be best for the entire global population to live in just one city? The answer is "not necessarily" because city life has certain limitations. Although these limits are constantly expanding, as seen in the growth of mega-cities, there comes a point when the cost in terms of time and money to commute to work becomes too high, and housing prices become too steep to be tolerable for living near economic activity centres. Nevertheless, it is evident that cities are the epicentres of economic activity and the main drivers of value creation.

Reykjavík in Winter, photo by the author

In Iceland, urbanisation characterised the 20th century with a rapid and dramatic transition. At the end of the 19th century, in 1890, 85% of the population lived in rural areas, while the urban area that would become Reykjavík had only 3,900 inhabitants. One hundred years later, 92% of Icelanders lived in urban areas,[25] making it one of the countries with the highest percentage of urban dwellers in the world. Out of these, approximately 70% resided in the capital area or within 100 kilometres of Reykjavík's centre. About 90% of the country's population growth in the first decade of the 21st century occurred in the capital area.[26] However, Iceland is a geographically large country with a low population density of about 3.1 inhabitants per square kilometre. It is similar to countries such as Australia and Canada, which also have vast and challenging-to-settle land areas. By comparison, Norway has 14 inhabitants per square kilometre, nearly five times more than Iceland, and the United Kingdom, Iceland's nearest southern neighbour, has 269 inhabitants per square kilometre, almost a hundred times more than Iceland.[27] If we focus solely on the seven municipalities in the capital area, the picture changes significantly, with a population density of about 200 people per square kilometre. This may not be dense on an international scale of metropolitan areas (London has a population density of almost 1,600 inhabitants per square kilometre), but it is still relatively high. If we exclude one of the largest yet sparsely populated municipalities, Kjósarhreppur, with around 200 inhabitants, the density increases to about 321 inhabitants per square kilometre. In 2023, there were 64 municipalities in Iceland with populations ranging from 47 to 140,000 inhabitants, but 45% of these municipalities had fewer than 1,000 inhabitants. [28] In neighbouring countries, such municipalities would be considered very small, and in some cases, they would not even be allowed.

3

Does Size Matter?

The relative size of the capital area in Iceland is highly unusual compared to the surrounding countries. Among the Nordic countries, Denmark has relatively the second largest capital area after Iceland, with approximately 36% of Danes residing in the Copenhagen area. The second largest urban area in Denmark, Aarhus, is home to about 15% of the population, while almost half of the Danish population (49%) lives outside these two metropolitan areas. In Sweden, around 23% of the population resides in the Stockholm area and about 10% in the Gothenburg area, while 67% of Swedes live in other urban or rural areas. The other Nordic countries fall somewhere in between, with Norway having around 30% of the population in the Oslo area and 8% in Bergen, and Finland having 26% in the Helsinki area and 7% in Tampere. Looking further south, London's population ranges from 8 to 16 million (depending on estimation methods), accounting for approximately 30% of England's population and 25% if the entire UK is considered. Even when compared to multi-core urban areas in Europe, none of them come close to the proportion of the population residing in the Reykjavík area, in which almost 64% of Icelanders reside. It is evident that Iceland, despite its population density, can be considered almost a city-state [29] [30] [31].

The significant size of the capital area in Iceland has led to a prominent urban-rural divide, which is a major issue in Icelandic politics. While this divide may not directly align with political party affiliations, there is a tendency for certain parties to garner support from specific regions. For example, the Progressive Party (Framsóknarflokkur) has historically sought support from rural areas, while the Social Democrats, (Alþýðuflokkur), and later The Social Democratic Alliance (Samfylkingin) have primarily sought support in urban areas, particularly in the southwest corner of the country, where the capital area is. This may reflect to some extent the ideologies and visions of these parties, with one focusing on the countryside and the other on urban areas. The Independence Party, although traditionally strong in Reykjavík, has seen its support shift to neighbouring municipalities as the capital area continues to grow. Despite its strength in the capital area, the party has always enjoyed support in rural areas as well.[32]

While the overwhelming size of the capital area in Iceland may create imbalances in terms of services and attractiveness for people and businesses, it also brings certain advantages. Considering the country's sparse population, the concentration of inhabitants in one city has significantly reduced emigration among Icelanders, unlike neighbouring Greenland and the Faroe Islands, where a considerable number of people, especially the educated, have migrated due to limited urbanisation.[33] Moreover, the capital area houses robust cultural and educational institutions that generate employment opportunities and drive Icelandic national culture together with servicing the rest of the country.[34]

Since the conclusion of World War II, the number of states has significantly grown as a result of the disintegration of empires and decolonisation, as well as the relatively stable global circumstances during that era. Starting with 45 member states at the establishment of the United Nations in 1945, the count reached 193 by its seventieth anniversary in 2015. A substantial portion of these newly formed states are categorised as small states, with Iceland serving as a prominent example due to its limited population.

However, it's important to note that population size alone does not exclusively determine the classification of small states. Factors such as international organisation memberships, economies, and other influences that may not correlate with population should also be considered.

As the capital of a state, Reykjavík often receives more attention and recognition in various contexts compared to cities of similar or even larger size that lack capital status. This attention can be both positive and negative, as exemplified by the global focus on Reykjavík during the 2008 financial crisis, which negatively impacted the city's reputation.[35]

Historically, Iceland was a remote agricultural region within the Kingdom of Denmark that implemented legislation against urbanisation, even as late as 1887 when laws were enacted to restrict settlement in specific areas without permission. The reasons behind this attitude among the ruling class can be debated, but one explanation may be their aversion to dealing with social issues that could arise in towns or from potentially unfavourable outcomes or in competition with the fishing industry for rural labour.[36]

However, the situation changed in the twentieth century, and the metropolitan Reykjavík area now boasts a population of over 245,000, accounting for more than 60% of the country's total. A significant portion of the country's population growth will likely occur in the city in the coming decades. Nonetheless, population projections by Statistics Iceland until 2060 suggest a more cautious increase. The country is experiencing an ageing population and declining birth rates, with the lowest migration balance among the Nordic countries. According to these projections, the Reykjavík area is expected to reach 300,000 inhabitants around 2095. The new master plan of the City of Reykjavík until 2030 also indicates a significant slowdown in population growth in the coming years, averaging around 0.9% per year, with a population of 300,000 projected by 2058.[37][38]

However, the question arises as to why the population size of cities matters, even at a minimum threshold of 100,000 inhabitants. Is there any significance in having a population of 200,000, 500,000, 1 million, 10 million, or 20 million? The forecasts of limited population growth in Reykjavík may not be encouraging news for the city, since research indicates that larger cities offer numerous advantages over smaller ones, particularly in terms of economy, social diversity, and infrastructure efficiency. Entrepreneurs often choose to establish their businesses in large cities, further contributing to prosperity, dynamism, and productivity. Studies consistently show a positive correlation between city size and average income, with productivity significantly higher in urban areas compared to rural regions. However, there are exceptions to this rule, as some cities that heavily relied on specific industries have suffered in terms of population and employment, as exemplified by Detroit's automotive industry or Manchester's declining industrial sector.[39] [40]

Urban planner Mario Polèse argues that larger cities generate higher relative revenue. This positive correlation between population size and income is well-known in regional economics, attributed to factors such as economies of scale in production and transportation, declining transportation costs, proximity benefits, diversity advantages, centralisation, and the vibrant atmosphere found in larger cities. Considering these factors, it may be beneficial for the Reykjavík area to attract more people and strive to avoid the gloomy predictions mentioned earlier. It is realistic to assume that a considerable number of individuals are willing to move to Reykjavík from other countries.[41]

4

Reykjavík in Comparison with Similar Cities

Reykjavík holds a unique position among cities as it is also the capital of Iceland. While modern international societies are not solely based on nation-states, these states remain the primary actors in the international arena, represented in international organisations, and responsible for agreements, passports, currencies, and defence.

Although Iceland is rarely mentioned in foreign media, when it is, there is more often than not a sentence about the Icelandic nation being "less populous than Bournemouth",[42] "able to fit on four football pitches",[43] or some similar attempt at a joke. However, Iceland holds a unique position compared to similarly land-rich countries where approximately 94% of Icelanders live in urban areas, with the majority residing in the capital area. This places Iceland among the nations with the highest percentage of urban population. In fact, Iceland ranks 19th globally in terms of urban population. It ranks there together with small island states in the Pacific and Caribbean, city-states in Europe or on the Arabian Peninsula, none of which have any hinterland to speak of. When excluding such states, only Belgium boasts a higher proportion of urban population globally than Iceland.[44]

It is evident that Reykjavík is not a large city on an international scale. Many of the cities that surpass Reykjavík in population we seldom hear mentioned nor is it likely we will visit many of them in our lifetimes. This leads to the question of whether this multitude of small and middle-sized cities offer the culture, business activity, and overall urban experience that we typically associate with bustling city life.

Determining the precise number of cities in the world is challenging, particularly when it comes to defining what qualifies as a city. Should all municipal divisions within urban areas be included? How small can a population be for an area to be considered a city? What level of population density is required? Various criteria, such as those provided by the website dbpedia.org, can be used to estimate the number of cities. Based on these criteria, there are approximately 2,900 cities worldwide with over one million inhabitants, around 4,250 cities with over half a million inhabitants, and roughly 6,500 cities with over 250,000 inhabitants. Therefore, it can be assumed that there are approximately 14,000 cities in the world that have a higher population than the capital area of Iceland. This presents an extensive basis for comparison.

Let's take Bournemouth as an example, as it has been mentioned here already. When comparing the statistics of Bournemouth and Reykjavík, these cities share many similarities despite Bournemouth being somewhat more populous. Bournemouth was first mentioned in written sources in 1406, although the reference was to the area where the city was later built, rather than an established urban settlement. Similar to Reykjavík, it wasn't until the 19th and 20th centuries that Bournemouth began to develop into a city. Bournemouth was granted city status in 1870. It currently has a population of over 180,000, or approximately 400,000 when including the surrounding area. It is home to two universities, a symphony orchestra founded in 1893, numerous restaurants, and nightclubs, and is a highly popular tourist destination, even more so than Reykjavík. Bournemouth has 26 primary schools and 10 secondary schools.[45] In comparison, the City of Reykjavík operates 36 primary schools, excluding neighbouring municipalities. Reykjavík has 10 secondary schools, while the entire capital area has 15. Additionally, Reykjavík has three universities and a symphony orchestra, founded in 1950.

Bournemouth is a vibrant city that attracts around 5 million tourists annually, nearly three times the number of tourists visiting Reykjavík. The city hosts numerous festivals each year, drawing a large number of people. It also has a high proportion of young people attending universities compared to the UK as a whole. Similar to Reykjavík, Bournemouth has embraced the annual Gay Pride celebration, which has become a significant event promoting diversity and solidarity. Bournemouth has a long-standing literary tradition dating back to the 19th and early 20th centuries, during which renowned writers, including J.R.R. Tolkien, author of The Hobbit and The Lord of the Rings, resided in the city for a significant proportion of his life.[46]

The Gay Pride Parade in August has become one of the largest annual events in Reykjavík. Here, Mayor Dagur B. Eggertsson (centre, with sunglasses) can be seen in a group of city councillors partaking in the parade in 2023. Photo by the author.

Despite all this, in its context, Bournemouth remains a secondary city at best, a city that is conveniently situated near the actual City itself, notably, London. Bournemouth is located about 180 km away from the bustling cosmopolitan centre. Anyhow, there are obvious similarities between Bournemouth and Reykjavík, although Bournemouth definitely enjoys a milder and friendlier climate.

Trondheim in Norway is another city comparable to Reykjavík in terms of population. Trondheim has the thirteenth largest metropolitan area in the Nordic countries (with the Reykjavík area being the fourteenth). The population of the Trondheim metropolitan area is approximately 280,000. About 180,000 people reside within the city of Trondheim itself. Trondheim, the district capital of Trøndelag, a county in the central part of Norway, is an ancient town by Nordic standards, dating back around a thousand years. It was previously known as Kaupangur and later as Niðarós. The city served as one of the main residences of the King of Norway until 1217. Trondheim housed an archbishopric, and its medieval influence on Iceland was significant, as Iceland fell within the extensive archbishopric, which also included the whole of Norway, Greenland, the Faroe Islands, Orkneys, Shetland, and the Isle of Man. Trondheim is home to a symphony orchestra, two universities, and eleven upper secondary schools, similar to Reykjavík in that regard. The city has a vibrant music and film scene and a significant proportion of young people, with students comprising about 20% of the population.[47]

Grenoble in France is another city relatively comparable in size to Reykjavík. The city itself has a population of almost 170,000, but its metropolitan or administrative area, despite being sparsely populated, is much more populous than the Reykjavík area, with approximately 400,000 people (similar to the whole of Iceland in fact).[48] Grenoble serves as the provincial capital of the Isère district in the Rhône-Alpes region, situated at the foot of the French Alps. Like the Reykjavík area, Grenoble's residents enjoy the proximity of magnificent nature, with towering alpine peaks reaching heights of 2500 to 3000 metres. This closeness to nature provides ample opportunities for tourism, sports, and outdoor activities, not unlike Reykjavík in that respect. The city traces its history back to the first century AD when it served as a Roman outpost in the region. In the 20th century, Grenoble developed a robust heavy industry linked to large-scale alpine power plants in the vicinity. The city hosted the tenth Winter Olympics in 1968, which spurred the development of extensive infrastructure, including airports, motorways, and modern ski resorts.

Grenoble University, established by papal decree in 1339, has since been divided into four relatively independent universities. These universities have gained international recognition and are at the forefront of research in mathematics, computer technology, and physics. Grenoble is also home to leading companies and scientists in biotechnology and nanotechnology. Additionally, it has the second-largest English-speaking community in France, following Paris.[49] The Rhône-Alpes region boasts the highest GDP per capita in France, outside of Paris.[50]

The three cities of Bournemouth, Trondheim, and Grenoble are Western European cities with slightly larger populations than Reykjavík. They share many similarities in terms of infrastructure, culture, and other factors that make cities fascinating as human settlements. An interesting observation is that all the aforementioned cities are home to universities, and could even be described as "university cities." The presence of a university in a city is one of the main conditions for growth, as stated by urban scientist Mario Polèse in his book "The Wealth and Poverty of Regions: Why Cities Matter" (2009). Polèse suggests that while it is possible for growing cities to attract universities, research strongly confirms the link between city growth and the existence of universities.[51] Universities attract "green" immigrants who often view these institutions as their primary workplaces. Moreover, universities draw students who adopt a particular lifestyle and demand services that contribute to making cities "hip and cool." Polèse asserts that although it is more challenging to demonstrate effects such as entrepreneurship and high-tech companies' relationship with universities, the rule of thumb is that the better the universities, the greater the impact. Consequently, "green" immigrants flock to cities where the best schools, bookstores, high-tech hospitals, research centres, and other scholarly resources are located. This phenomenon in part explains the growth of cities like Boston, San Francisco, and New York.

On the other hand, universities do not gain prestige overnight; it takes decades, even centuries, to build their reputation.[52] Edward Glaeser, in his book "The Triumph of the City",[53] highlights that, apart from average temperatures in January, the level of education, especially among those a little into adulthood, is the most reliable predictor of urban growth. Per capita productivity experiences a significant boost with city size if the residents are well-educated, but not if they are not. This demonstrates the interplay between good schools and successful cities, making education policy a key factor in a city's prosperity.[54] To strengthen Reykjavík as a university city, a feasible step would be for the University of Iceland to significantly expand its English-language study programs. Currently, the university's effort in this regard has been lacking, with international student numbers (including exchange students) increasing by only 64% since the beginning of the 21st century, from 411 in 2000 to 1,549 in the 2019-20 academic year.[55] This growth is surprisingly modest, considering the overall increase in the student population and the rising immigration to the country. It can be assumed that attracting individuals who could contribute to Icelandic society in the long run would be possible by offering relevant programs at the University of Iceland, by far its largest university and an institution that enjoys a relatively good international reputation.

Over the past 25 years, European universities have significantly increased their cooperation and coordination, particularly through the so-called "Bologna Process". The Bologna Process, established in 1999 through an agreement signed at the University of Bologna, involved 29 European countries, including Iceland. It aimed to harmonise study programs and ensure comparable degree requirements across European universities. This led Icelandic universities to focus on enhancing their quality through regular evaluations by foreign experts. As a result, there has been a substantial influx of European students and teachers, along with increased research collaboration funded by the European Union. Icelandic universities are now intimately connected to the European university network, granting students degrees and credits recognised throughout Europe and, thus, most of the world. This should enable Icelandic universities to attract a larger share of global university students, positively affecting the cities hosting them.

(Mynd af HÍ)

The three cities mentioned earlier, compared to Reykjavík, are all desirable places to live, study, and work, although not all cities are as attractive. Reykjavík is not included on the website citymayors.com, which lists the 500 largest cities in Europe. The list features both well-known and lesser-known cities. The last city on the list is Norilsk, a Russian city with around 149,000 inhabitants. Norilsk holds the distinction of being the northernmost city in the world with over 100,000 inhabitants, located at 69°20'N and 88°13'E, which is even further north than Akureyri at 65.7'N, and well above the Arctic Circle at 66°N. Norilsk was established in the 1930s on a rich nickel mine in the Siberian permafrost, and mining remains its primary industry. Approximately 20% of the world's nickel comes from Norilsk, making it a significant contributor to Russia's GDP. However, the city is also one of the most polluted in the world, with the winter snow bearing the marks of its industrial activities. Norilsk's history includes a dark period of forced labour during the Soviet era, with numerous deaths occurring in the city's mines, including over 16,000 people between 1935 and 1956, mostly during World War II. Notably, Nadezhda Andreyevna Tolokonnikova, a member of the Russian punk band Pussy Riot, hails from Norilsk. Norilsk has a university named Fedorovsky Polar State University. The city is highly isolated, with only one railway connecting it to the port city of Dudinka. Travel options include a 2,000 km journey down the Yenisei River or air travel with potentially significant delays due to adverse weather conditions.

The aforementioned list also includes other European cities larger than Reykjavík but with populations below 200,000. These cities, such as Neuss in Germany, Macclesfield in the United Kingdom, Ruda Slaska in Poland, and Basel in Switzerland, are seldom in the news. However, well-known cities like Geneva, York, Parma, Salamanca, Leverkusen, and Lille are also on the list.

Looking beyond Europe, there are numerous cities the size of Reykjavík or larger. Many of these cities serve as provincial capitals in their respective countries, such as Arusha in Tanzania, with a population of approximately 400,000. Arusha is the tourism hub of northern Tanzania, boasting remarkable natural wonders like Mt. Kilimanjaro, Serengeti, Tarangire, and Ngorongoro National Parks. It sits on the edge of the vast African Rift Valley and was initially established around 1830 as a trading centre for the local tribes. The city came under German control in 1896 and subsequently grew when the British captured it towards the end of World War I. Today, Arusha serves as a regional service centre and hosts international organisations like the East African Community, as well as multinational tribunals such as the Rwandan Tribunal and the African Court on Human and Peoples' Rights. The city has an international airport and several schools, including universities, and, due to its high altitude of 1400 metres, enjoys a temperate climate despite its proximity to the equator.

In Europe, there exists an economic growth corridor known as the "blue crescent" or "blue banana." This expansive region stretches from Manchester in the north to Milan in the south, encompassing Europe's most industrialised and prosperous areas, including the Netherlands, the Rhine region, and Switzerland. Within this corridor lies a densely populated zone with significant industrial activity and modern infrastructure, boasting a population of approximately 111 million. [56] Studies indicate that outside the blue crescent, in countries such as those in Central and Eastern Europe, the wealthiest and most industrialised regions tend to be located in the western parts of those countries closest to the blue crescent. Conversely, the easternmost regions of neighbouring countries usually experience higher levels of poverty.

Europe's national borders have had a profound impact on the development of cities across the continent, resulting in smaller urban centres compared to what may have emerged if the circumstances were similar to those in the relatively borderless United States. In such a scenario, a few large cities might have arisen, likely within the blue crescent or its immediate vicinity. However, Reykjavík, situated on an island at a considerable distance from its nearest neighbouring country, follows a distinct trajectory. The development of Reykjavík would probably have taken a different course had Iceland, in the twentieth century, been part of another country where governance remained centred in a distant capital, such as Copenhagen, Oslo, or London. The scenarios that are most likely to have occurred.

The Netherlands would be considered almost entirely within the blue crescent. The state's administrative capital is The Hague, and there are also many international organisations, including the International Court of Justice (ICJ), which is the main court of the United Nations and settles international disputes that states choose to refer to it. It also houses the International Criminal Court (ICC), as well as courts on local conflicts in the former Yugoslavia and Rwanda. The Hague is the fourth major administrative centre of the United Nations, as well as being home to the Dutch parliament and ministries.

The Hague is not a very big city, with a population of about 500,000, but it is almost fully adjacent to the city of Rotterdam, so the metropolitan area of these two cities (which currently contain many smaller municipalities) has a population of 2.2 million. These cities are then part of the Randstad, which includes the four largest cities in the Netherlands, Amsterdam, Rotterdam, The Hague and Utrecht, as well as their suburbs, in which almost seven million of the 17 million people who live in the Netherlands reside.

It must therefore be said that the whole framework of city life is different in The Hague than in Reykjavík, with its 245 thousand inhabitants, and the infrastructure stronger. However, they do not necessarily have to be more efficient- but they certainly are! The Hague has a dense network of public transport. Within the city limits, it is the trams that make the biggest impression. Rarely do you have to wait more than ten minutes for the next carriage and large signs at each stop indicate when the next one will arrive. When you go further into the suburbs, newer light rail trains take over, as well as traditional buses. Between the cities, there are the trains that transport people between large, bright train stations that are most often full of well-dressed people with briefcases or small bags on their way to work in one of the ministries, international organisations or the many businesses or shops in the city. There are also students on the way to or from school, but they get to ride the trains for free while they are studying and thus use them a lot.

Centraal Station in The Hague, photo by the author.

However, it is not the powerful public transport that is most interesting when it comes to commuting in The Hague. It is the fact that an unusually high percentage of the city's residents use bicycles every day to commute, as the city is probably one of the best in the world when it comes to infrastructure for cyclists. On almost every main street there are special lanes for bicycles and the fact that car drivers take them into account in all respects makes this mode of transport one of the most convenient in the city. It is also relatively densely populated so you can get to most of the places you want in about 20 minutes, and it takes 45 minutes to cycle from one end of the city to the other.[57]

Bikes come in all shapes and sizes, from small folding bikes to giant family bikes with wooden front or rear carriages where people store their children, sometimes 2-3 together, and ride them to and from school. Precious few cyclists wear bicycle helmets, and it takes some time for those accustomed to strict helmet use and more dangerous city traffic to get over the shock of this sight, to see parents with their children without helmets in small carriages or fixed seats, riding beside buses, trams and trucks. However, due to the well-designed cycle path system, well demarcated from car traffic and the aforementioned consideration of drivers, the risk of this behaviour seems to be negligible.[58]

The Hague is certainly a flat city. There are no slopes to speak of, as it is below sea level, based on a flat, dry seabed. The climate in winter, however, is no better than on frost-free winter days in Reykjavík. The saying "If you don't like the weather, wait five minutes" is as widely used in The Hague as in the northernmost capital of the world. The wind destroys umbrellas instantly and the rain is horizontal, just like in Reykjavík, as the city is open to strong north and west winds from the North Sea and icy continental winds all the way east from Siberia itself. Despite this weather, it is a common practice to fight through the city in large human turfs on bikes. And the lack of a helmet makes cycling as natural and easy as walking. No special equipment is required. No bad hair and spandex shorts. Just jump on the bike in your suit and ride to work.

The Hague shares an airport with Rotterdam, but it is a secondary airport to the magnificent international transport hub, Schiphol Airport, which is only 40 minutes and 8 euros away by train, and where people can travel in dry clothes from two city train stations to jump on the planes that take off constantly 24 hours a day, to all corners of the world.

For the most part, it is unfair to compare the detached Reykjavík with a city in the middle of a metropolitan area of 7 million people; and within the blue crescent, but the tram and cycling system is certainly something that could be taken into account as a model for how transport within the city can be made efficient. Trams have the advantage, in addition to being an environmentally friendly mode of transport, (they run on electricity of course), to establish permanent transport arteries and thus solidify the neighbourhoods in the vicinity of the stops. Investors and others who want to establish themselves there can expect that in the long term, there will be reliable and safe public transport in their neighbourhood and connections to all transport networks in the city area. In such an environment, the private car becomes virtually unnecessary. Something to use on Sundays when going out to the countryside to visit grandparents. Or when you need to buy furniture at IKEA or shop food for the week in the supermarket.

So, the weather can be bad in other cities of the world, and still, people cycle to work and take the bus. But, is the weather anywhere as bad as it is in Reykjavík? Let's turn to that question.

II

Environment, History, and Planning

5

Nature and Climate

The climate in Reykjavík has a poor reputation. That is justified. There are years when it feels like summer never arrives. For example, the summers of 2013, 2014, 2021, and 2022 were considered "bad" summers due to fewer hours of sunshine than in a "normal" year. In July, the hottest month, the average temperature ranges from 9.4 to 15.2 degrees Celsius (°C). The highest temperature recorded in Reykjavík in July was 24.8°C in August 2004.[59] In January, the coldest month, the average temperature ranges from two degrees above zero to three degrees below zero, with a record low of almost twenty degrees below zero (-19.7 °C) in 1971.[60] Such temperatures are however quite rare in Reykjavík. In his book "The Triumph of the City," Edward Glaeser highlights that January temperatures are a significant predictor of urban growth, making it a variable worth considering.[61]

Compared to cities like Trondheim in Norway and Norilsk in Siberia, Reykjavíkians have less to complain about than they think. While these cities generally have warmer summers in terms of temperature, the average winter temperature in

Trondheim is similar to Reykjavík, around -1.2 °C, whereas it drops to -27 °C in Norilsk. Trondheim also enjoys around 10 more hours of sunshine in July compared to Reykjavík, but it experiences about one-third more rainfall on average during that month.

Suppose we shift our focus to cities in the southern parts of the continent. In that case, there is a significant difference in average temperatures between Reykjavík and Grenoble in France or Bournemouth in the United Kingdom, making summers in those cities much more pleasant. In July, Grenoble has an average temperature ranging from 14 to 26°C, while Bournemouth has an average temperature of 12 to 22°C. However, the difference is not as pronounced when considering the important variable of January temperature. In January, the average temperature in Grenoble ranges from -1 to 6 degrees Celsius, and in Bournemouth, which has milder winters than Grenoble, it ranges from 1.5 to 8.4°C. The temperature in Grenoble fluctuates more than in Reykjavík, with the coldest measurement recorded at -27.1°C in January. In comparison, the lowest temperature in Bournemouth was -13°C.

Iceland has an oceanic climate due to its global position in the middle of the North Atlantic. The average temperature at the latitude where Reykjavík is located, approximately 64° N, is around -18°C in January and 15°C in July. Comparatively, Reykjavík experiences an average temperature of around 0°C in January and 11°C in July. This significant difference can be attributed to the impact of the ocean surrounding the island in the north.[62] The British Isles and the northern coast of mainland Europe are also influenced by this factor. Although temperatures in these regions are generally higher than in Iceland, they are not extremely high, nor very cold in winter, although freezing temperatures can occur. For example, in The Hague, Netherlands, the weather in January is characterised by rain and wind, with an average temperature ranging from 1°C to almost 6°C. July weather is more pleasant with an average temperature between 13°C and 21°C.[63]

Over the past century, the weather has improved in Reykjavík. To some extent, this can be attributed to the fact that the Reykjavík area has become the largest forest in the country in terms of size and area, but of course, this refers to all the tree plants that grow in the city's gardens, in open areas within the city, as well as the so-called "green scarf." This green scarf is an area around the city where massive forestry has taken place over the past century. The name was used for the common forestry of the municipalities in the capital area from the 1990s, and it is said that winds and weather conditions have changed significantly with its introduction, making the Reykjavík area both calmer and warmer than before.[64]

Heiðmörk, a conservation area within the Green Scarf surrounding Reykjavík, contributes to a milder climate in the city than before. Photo by the author.

The Gulf Stream is vital for Reykjavík's climate, making it much warmer and more consistent throughout the year compared to most other cities at a similar latitude. However, Reykjavík is also known for being very windy, especially during the winter, due to its location on the path of low-pressure systems as they cross the Atlantic. Recently, there has been concern about a slowdown in the Gulf Stream due to increased freshwater flow into the North Atlantic caused by the melting of Greenland ice, which is linked to climate change. If the Gulf Stream were to halt, it would have negative consequences for Reykjavík, Iceland, and Northern Europe as a whole.[65]

In Iceland, the weather is largely influenced by the position and movement of meteorological systems, specifically high and low-pressure systems. Iceland lies within one of the two main semi-permanent low-pressure systems in the northern hemisphere, known as the Icelandic Low. This system, along with the prevailing winds, contributes to the windiness of Iceland, with the western wind belt near Antarctica being the only windier area on Earth. Rainfall in Iceland is relatively common, although it usually occurs in smaller quantities and is often accompanied by strong winds.[66]

Reykjavík, being the capital city, is closest to the Arctic among all capital cities in the world, making it one of the windiest capitals as well. However, there are significant climatic differences within Iceland and even within the capital area. The growing season in the south of Iceland is considerably longer than in the Westfjords and the north of Iceland. Precipitation also varies, with Reykjavík receiving an average of about 800 mm of rainfall per year, while Akureyri, in the north, receives around 490 mm. The prevailing wind direction plays a crucial role in determining daily weather conditions, with land winds being dry and slightly cloudy, while sea winds bring clouds and rain. The wind systems in Reykjavík vary throughout the day, with sea breezes from the northwest during the day and land breezes from the east and south at night.[67]

The old town in Reykjavík is a low-density urban area akin to a small village. Photo by the author.

The wind in urban areas is often perceived negatively due to its cooling effect and its ability to carry rain, dust, sand, and snow, causing inconveniences and challenges for residents. However, wind also helps to regulate temperature and humidity, dilute air pollution, and is increasingly seen as a potential environmentally friendly energy resource in Iceland. The impact of high winds on buildings, particularly high-rise structures, has sparked controversies in Reykjavík. Low-density urban areas, such as the old town of Reykjavík and the centre of Hafnarfjörður, create more favourable weather conditions as the wind tends to settle down between the buildings.[68]

One of Reykjavík's unique features is the widespread access to geothermal hot water. Since the early 20th century, houses in Reykjavík have been heated with geothermal energy, and this practice expanded to all residential buildings in the capital area during the 1970s. The abundance of hot water also contributes to the high quality of life in Reykjavík, with numerous heated swimming pools and hot tubs available for health and recreational purposes. Reykjavík can in fact be considered a "spa city," boasting close to twenty public swimming pools, including the famous Blue Lagoon, just 33.5 km from the city's outskirts. Swimming pools are highly popular among both locals and tourists, with approximately two million visitors annually. While some tourists may be surprised by the requirement to shower naked before entering the pool, swimming pools receive the highest satisfaction rating among the attractions Iceland has to offer.[69][70]

6

A Danish Outpost

Despite the weather, it can be said that the people of Iceland have never truly accepted not living in mainland Europe. In some ways that is understandable. Despite its high latitude, the vegetation in Iceland, at least in the habitable areas, is actually more similar to the temperate regions of northwestern Europe, such as Scandinavia and the British Isles, than Arctic regions like its nearest neighbour, Greenland.[71] Settlers from the mainland brought their farming practices with them, and housing in the early centuries of the settlement was based on what they knew from Norway and the British Isles rather than considering the specific climatic conditions in Iceland. The most tragic examples of such miscalculations are undoubtedly the large cathedrals in Skálholt and Hólar, which were built from wood and were at the time the most extensive timber structures in Europe. They were simply blown away by the winter storms.[72] However, sod housing was an effort to adapt to the extreme weather conditions.

Reykjavík was a named settlement mentioned in Landnáma (The Book of Settlements from the Middle Ages), and it is known as the site of the "first settler," Ingólfur Arnarson. It was initially divided into many settlements,[73] and other parts of the country made efforts to develop urban areas. Places like Vestmannaeyjar, Grindavík, Hafnarfjörður, as well as the bishoprics Skálholt and Hólar, engaged in various activities such as schooling, trade, handicrafts, printing, and church administration. There was no indication in the Middle Ages that the alleged first settlement would later become the leading force in the urban development of Iceland. However, it does not take much research to see that the Reykjavík area is actually the best location in the country for a city. It is a large plain with easy access to the sea and excellent sites for harbours. The climate is mild all year round and sea ice is very rare, and, despite proximity to a volcanically active area on the Reykjanes peninsula, it is not really threatened by any impending natural disasters, like floods, strong earthquakes, avalanches, mudslides or volcanic eruptions, all of which are real and significant threats to urban settlements in other parts of the country.

A factory village began to emerge in Reykjavík following the initiative of Skúli Magnússon, the highest official in the country at the time, to establish industry in that place. Machinery and equipment were brought from abroad in the summer of 1752 for a weaving factory, accompanied by permanent residents. The village survived the bankruptcy of the factory a few decades later.[74]

The next significant step was taken when a royal committee, which was tasked with examining various developments in Iceland between 1785 and 1794, proposed the lifting of the trading monopoly enjoyed by the Danish monarchy and the establishment of a few towns in the country. On August 18, 1786, town rights were granted to six places: Reykjavík,

Grundarfjörður, Ísafjarðarbær, Akureyri, Eskifjörður, and the Westman Islands. Town rights were special privileges enjoyed by urban areas according to the law, allowing them to engage in trade and industry and have a separate town council from the surrounding county administration. However, the development of these new towns in Iceland did not go as planned, and except for Reykjavík, their town rights, expired in 1836.[75]

Reykjavík 1835 – Drawing by Joseph Gaimard

At that time, Iceland was part of the Danish-Norwegian kingdom. It is interesting to consider the settlement patterns in other parts of the kingdom at that time. In Denmark itself, the church played a major role in the development of urban areas, similar to Hólar and Skálholt in Iceland, where urban areas developed around bishoprics such as Ribe, Århus, Odense, and Roskilde. Other places developed for secular reasons, such as being close to transportation and resources or being of military importance, like Viborg and Ringsted. Urban development in Denmark was slow in the 11th and 12th centuries, but it picked up with increased activity in the Baltic Sea, and many towns were established in the 14th and 15th centuries. However, these times were not conducive to urban development due to the impact of the Black Death pandemic.[76]

It can be said that urban development in Denmark did not fully recover after the Black Death until the second half of the 19th century with the onset of industrialisation. In Jutland, most towns were port towns, while only three inland towns were relatively close to the sea and engaged in sea trade. The towns became administrative centres with the division of the country in 1662. Towns in Jutland remained rural villages until the 19th century. Unlike what was in more southern parts of mainland Europe, no city walls were built around Danish towns, and the construction of houses was not very different from what took place in rural areas. The defining characteristic of a town was primarily its aforementioned privileges, the town rights. Towns often had one or two parallel streets or one crossroads, known as Bredgade (Broad Street) and Algade (Main Street). The houses were single-story, without foundations, thatched roofs, few or no windows, and no chimneys except for a hole in the ceiling. Larger houses resembled farmhouses with gates, and only the most significant and largest towns had half-timbered two-story houses or brick houses.[77]

Urbanisation was slower in Sweden and Finland compared to Denmark and Norway. By the year 1100, many medieval towns had already been established in Denmark and Norway, while only two towns, Lödöse and Skara, existed in Götaland, Sweden, and one, Sigtuna, in the rest of Sweden. It took 200 years before towns began to emerge inland to some extent in Sweden, and peripheral Finland was even further behind in development. In 1500, there were six towns in Finland, with only Åbo (or Turku) existing in 1300. In contrast, the Kingdom of Denmark had around 100 towns by 1500, with about a third of them located in what is now Sweden and 15 in Norway. These towns were relatively small compared to European standards and primarily served as craft centres and regional markets.[78]

Cities, however, began to take shape with significant urban activity around the Kattegat Strait by the end of the sixteenth century. The name Kattegat actually means "Cat's Gate" and allegedly comes about because of its shallow seas and narrow waterways, where even a cat would have difficulty squeezing through![79] At the time, Copenhagen had a population of about 20,000 people, Malmö had around 6,000, and Helsingør had around 5,000 inhabitants. In Uppsala, located in Fjärdhundraland, the population was about 5,000 people. In Jutland, Aalborg had between 5,000 and 6,000 inhabitants, while Aarhus and Ribe had around 4,500 inhabitants each.[80]

During this time, the legal code focused on town and city life, particularly the hygiene of the streets. Provisions were made to ensure that the street owners kept the streets clean from their dwellings to the centre of the street. Such regulations can be traced back as early as 1268 in Roskilde and 1531 in Ålborg. Laws were also enacted concerning culverts from houses and pig pens, indicating that cities were expected to be relatively clean by that time. There was a noticeable trend toward planning houses, wells, gardens, and covering culverts and drains under the law.[81]

Copenhagen's period of rapid growth was only just beginning. Between 1672 and 1769, the population in rural towns grew by only 5%, while Copenhagen's population increased by 129%. This slow urban growth in Denmark outside the capital reflected broader European trends, albeit on a smaller scale.[82] Denmark's social structure in the Middle Ages was predominantly agricultural, and the commercial activities of the peasantry did not encourage significant urban development. The existing towns were secondary and marginalised in the social structure, as rural life was self-sufficient.[83]

In Norway, which was also part of the Danish Kingdom when Reykjavík began to form as a village, urban settlements had already begun to emerge during the early Middle Ages, with settlements concentrated in the western parts of the country. The Norse settlement of Iceland, Greenland, the Faroe Islands, and the British Isles was concluded at that time, and ancient places of worship and gatherings started to evolve into urban centres. At the end of the eleventh century, bishoprics such as Tønsberg, Sarpsborg, Hamar, and Stavanger, which served as trading posts, took on the appearance of cities. The most important cities were the provincial capitals of Niðarós (Trondheim), Oslo, and Bergen. Niðarós, with its archbishopric and the remains of Saint Olaf, the nation's founding father and patron saint, was the spiritual centre of the state during the Middle Ages. Oslo, an ancient trading post, experienced relative decline in the early Middle Ages. Bergen, a major trading city and a central location on the Norwegian coast, thrived due to its trade in dried fish and became the largest city in Northern Europe at the time. However, Bergen's growth was limited by its steep slopes. Other cities in Norway were relatively rural villages, as most of the country's population consisted of farmers.[84]

The 14th and 15th centuries marked a period of decline in Norway. The Hanseatic merchants became active, and Norway went through various unions with Sweden, Denmark, and both, ultimately returning to Danish rule. Norway was always the less important party in these relationships. The Black

Death pandemic ravaged the country, and the Reformation further weakened the bishoprics and their property. Trade and commerce gradually declined, except for the trade in cod, haddock, and timber, which remained in demand in Europe. The 17th century saw the emergence of a bourgeoisie in Norway, laying the foundation for later urbanisation.[85]

In Sweden, Stockholm served as the capital then, as it does now. Stockholm was founded in the mid-thirteenth century as a trading place for goods from the surrounding areas of Lake Mälaren and Bergslagen. It played a similar role on the east coast of the Scandinavian Peninsula as Bergen did on the west coast. By the end of the Middle Ages, Stockholm's population was about 7,000, making it the largest city in Sweden at that time, comparable in size to Bergen. However, only five other towns in Sweden had reached a population of 1,000. Nordic cities, though small on a European scale, played a significant economic role as centres for production, trade, and government. They were places where new ideas and the latest fashions in clothing, arts, and crafts were spread. Farmers, hunters, aristocrats, and others brought their surplus goods to these cities, often selling directly to consumers. These marketplaces facilitated the exchange of goods even across long distances, extending as far as Iceland.[86]

In the late Middle Ages, German merchants gained dominance in the Baltic Sea trade and acted as intermediaries for Scandinavian products in the European market. Nordic merchants faced challenges in selling their goods and were nearly excluded from trade with England. During the early 14th century, fish, both dried and salted, emerged as Scandinavia's most important export product. However, the devastating impact of the Black Death pandemic severely affected this trade, and it was not until the late 16th century that trade reached similar levels again. Norway's primary export to the English market was fish, while lard, derived from cod, trout, seals, and whales, was another significant export product used mainly for lighting and leather tanning. Wood and leather goods also played a role in exports. Additionally, goods such as butter, falcons, whetstones, tar, and wool were marketed in southern Europe during the early 14th century.[87]

Danes did not export much to England; instead, they primarily traded with the Netherlands, Lübeck, and other German cities, exporting butter, cattle, hides, and horses. Swedes exported iron, copper, butter, and skins, mainly from Stockholm but also from other towns along the east coast. Scandinavians mainly imported grain and wheat from the Baltic Sea region, beer from Germany, salt from Lüneburg, and clothing from England and Flanders. The typical shipping route involving Norwegian ports near Bergen carried grain, wheat, and beer from the Baltic ports, then dried cod from Norway was transported to England or Flanders and then the ships returned to the Baltic Sea harbours with clothing.[88]

During the Middle Ages, Scandinavia was divided into three economic regions. Firstly it was Denmark, with its fertile core and overproduction of goods easily transported by land or short sea routes. The region also had abundant fishing grounds near the coast, attracting foreign traders with various goods. Within Denmark, an active economy utilizing currency in trade thrived, with weekly markets held in most towns. Secondly, in contrast, most Norwegians and Swedes lived on subsistence farms and had little surplus after paying taxes and rent, making it challenging for them to participate in the market. Markets in Norway were usually seasonal, and few Norwegians could attend in a single day. Thirdly, certain regions in Norway and Sweden, mostly in the high north, produced goods that fetched good prices in foreign markets, leading to prosperity and significant "international" trade. Accounts from foreigners shipwrecked in these areas describe the better quality of life there compared to most Europeans, even though dried fish was used as a form of currency.[89] In economic terms, settlements in Iceland likely shared many similarities with these resource-rich northern regions of Scandinavia during this period.

In the early days of the settlement period, Iceland's main exports were destined for Norway, specifically the city of Bergen. However, in the 14th century, the Norwegian Empire declined, and Hanseatic merchants took over most of Norway's trade. The centre of power shifted south to Copenhagen, resulting in a collapse of Norwegian shipping to Iceland and the loss of the lifeline Norway had provided to the island. The English quickly filled this void and began extensive voyages to Iceland in the early 15th century. The processing methods of fish in Iceland differed from those of the Norwegians. While the English had been the primary purchaser of Icelandic fish in Bergen, German Hanseatic merchants, who preferred the Norwegian variety, drove the English out of Bergen and thus the English started sailing to this island in the north, where they could obtain the kind of fish they desired.[90]

In 1397 Eric of Pomerania, the Danish king, assumed control over all the Nordic countries through the Kalmar Union. Dissatisfied with the English presence in Iceland, the king sent letters to the islanders prohibiting trade with the English and at the same time lodged complaints with the English king through a delegation to his court. In 1419, Icelanders wrote a letter to the king, referring to the Old Covenant signed when they joined Norway in 1262 to support their case of trade with the English and citing that the ships promised by the king in that covenant from Norway had not been forthcoming, seriously harming "this poor land" and thus the English trade was in their view quite welcome. The letter, bearing a total of 24 seals, was signed by correspondents, including the country's main rulers, Arnfinnur Þorsteinsson, two lawyers named Rafn and Oddur, and 19 others.[91] Despite the king's prohibitions and complaints, they had little impact in Iceland since he in fact lacked the ability to enforce his will in this faraway land.[92]

7

The Birth of a Capital

If there were any other place besides Reykjavík that could have become the capital of the country, it is evident that Hafnarfjörður would have made a strong contender. The centre of Hafnarfjörður is approximately 9 km away from the centre of Reykjavík in a straight line. Today, Hafnarfjörður is undeniably a part of the Reykjavík area, although one needs to cross three municipal boundaries to travel between the two municipalities. As the name suggests, the port conditions in Hafnarfjörður (Harbour Bay) are favourable. As early as the early fifteenth century, the town had established itself as an export port where the English purchased dried cod. The first merchant ship, reportedly sailing to Hafnarfjörður, arrived in 1413.[93] Hanseatic merchants began voyaging to Hafnarfjörður in 1468 and engaged in a conflict with the English over the location. Ultimately, the Germans emerged victorious, although their success was attributed more to a diverse range of products rather than physical or military superiority over the English. By the sixteenth century, Hafnarfjörður had become the primary port for Hanseatic merchants in Iceland.

Hafnarfjörður is a very pretty part of the capital area and has a long and illustrious history as a trading port since medieval times. Photo by the author.

Various factors contributed to Hafnarfjörður losing its prominence to Reykjavík. Some believe that the main reason lies in Skúli Magnússon choosing Reykjavík as the site for the company *Det Privilegerte Islandske Interessentskab*, (The Privileged Icelandic Company) or "Innréttingarnar" as it was usually called in Icelandic, thereby propelling the town to the forefront of the country's small-scale industrialisation. Others argue that Hafnarfjörður's lack of lowland compared to Reykjavík played a role. However, it can be concluded that this alone would not have significantly altered the current settlement pattern, as Hafnarfjörður is situated in the same region as Reykjavík and the town is now simply a part of the city, albeit with its own separate town council.

Other notable places in the Reykjavík area have played significant roles in the country's development since its time as part of the Norwegian Kingdom. Bessastaðir, located between the old town of Reykjavík and Hafnarfjörður, served as the seat of the royal governor and later the administration of the King of Denmark, governors, and county officials until the seat of government was moved to Reykjavík. From 1805, the most important school in Iceland, Hólavallaskóli (later renamed Bessastaðaskóli), was located there, establishing the capital area as the country's primary educational centre.[94] The decision to relocate Hólavallaskóli from Skálholt to Reykjavík in 1785-1786 is regarded as one of the most impactful choices in the country's history. The school is still in operation today under the name *Menntaskólinn í Reykjavík*, or Reykjavík Junior College. Bessastaðir subsequently became the residence of the head of state, the President of Iceland, following the establishment of the republic in 1944.

Another important place in the capital area that has lost its former significance is the island of Viðey just outside Reykjavík harbour. A monastery existed in Viðey from 1225, but it closed its doors in the wake of the Reformation in the 16th century. In 1752-1755, Viðeyjarstofa, a house that still stands on the island, was constructed as the official residence of the governor of Iceland. For several decades, the island was home to the most influential individuals in the country, including Ólafur Stephensen, the first governor of Icelandic birth, and his son Magnús Stephensen, a conference councillor and judge. At the beginning of the twentieth century, a small village was established on the island, centred around fishing activities with a population of 138 souls by 1930. However, the village suffered from the bankruptcy of the local fishing company, leading to its complete abandonment in 1943.[95] Today, very little remains of the village, but the island is now a nature reserve and houses the two old buildings: Viðeyjarstofa, which is run as a museum and a restaurant and Viðeyjarkirkja (the church). Viðey is also the site for the "Imagine Peace Tower" a work of art conceived by the artist Yoko Ono as a beacon for world peace. It is composed of a number of individual lights that join together to form a single beam into the night sky. It is illuminated every year from 9 October in celebration of John Lennon's birthday to the day of his assassination 8 December. It is also lit during the Christmas period and on two other occasions in the spring.

The history of Reykjavík has been extensively documented in numerous books. Several television and radio shows, such as by Egill Helgason, Lísa Pálsdóttir and Hjálmar Sveinsson, have highlighted various aspects of the urban area's development in the capital region. Notable historians such as Eggert Þór Bernharðsson and Guðjón Friðriksson, as well as writers like Halldór Laxness, Ásta Sigurðardóttir, Einar Már Guðmundsson, Pétur Guðmundsson, Einar Kárason, Helgi Ingólfsson, Ármann Jakobsson, Yrsa Sigurðardóttir and Arnaldur Indriðason, have contributed to these narratives, which often centres around the Reykjavík bourgeoisie, as they constituted the core of power in the city and exerted the greatest influence on its development. This social group comprised merchants, shipowners, and officials who constructed grand villas in Vesturbær and on the south and west sides of Þingholt. Artists, writers, intellectuals, and even schoolboys who left their mark on the town, especially after the establishment of the Reykjavík Junior College on the hill above the stream in 1846, are also frequently mentioned.

During the second half of the nineteenth century, civil society began to take shape, driven by the growing fishing, trade, and small-scale industries, as well as the burgeoning independence movement. Any doubts about Reykjavík's leadership in Iceland's development were put to rest. Reykjavík had established itself as the undeniable capital city.

8

Concrete and Parking Spots

Despite its early origins, Reykjavík is a 20th-century city. It is sprawled out, and its districts bear the characteristics of the prevailing zeitgeist during their construction. Consequently, the old town has an organic feel akin to villages from eras past. It extends up the slopes from the harbour, which serves as its heart and gateway. In chapter 8 of the 12th Century "Book of Settlement", one of Ingólfur Arnarson's slaves is quoted, "For evil we went about a good district, that we shall settle on this islet," referring to the chosen location for the settlement, after having traversed through the more fertile looking south of the country.[96] Undoubtedly, this area forms the old heart of the city on the headland. When examining a map of the Reykjavík area today, it becomes evident that it has a crescent shape around Skerjafjörður, with the headland prominently featured. Surrounding the headland, residential areas, industrial zones, and shopping districts were developed based on twentieth-century ideas of modern urban spaces, where the private car played a central role in the organisation.

In just a few decades, significant progress has been made in reimagining Reykjavík as a space that fosters diverse human life and offers alternative modes of transportation beyond relying solely on cars. There was a time when such a notion was nearly non-existent, as the entire city was organized around private cars. The City of Reykjavík's website highlights this transformation, stating, "Too much of the city's land is dedicated to streets and transportation infrastructure. Up to 48% of the urban areas in the city are allocated to traffic. Similar percentages are only found in most car-dependent cities in the United States and Australia. This means that over 80% of the open spaces between houses in the city are used for transportation."[97] The fact that this information is now posted on the city's website indicates a shift in thinking compared to the past. The text continues, "The master plan 2010-2030 presents a fresh perspective on streets in the city plan. New concepts are introduced, such as city streets and main streets, emphasizing the multifaceted role of streets in urban society. City streets are the primary streets of each neighbourhood, prioritised for redesign and beautification as public spaces accommodating all modes of transport."[98]

Recently, the municipalities in the capital area have collaborated on a comprehensive plan for the region known as the regional plan. The introductory text of this plan highlights the following:

> *The capital area presents a multifaceted economy driven by creativity and resourcefulness. It thrives on solid foundations of value generation, resulting in wages and living standards that rival the best globally. The region's research institutions occupy leading positions, serving as the bedrock for fruitful innovation across various*

fields. Greater Reykjavík embodies the essence of a contemporary urban community, blending international influences with distinct local characteristics. This dynamic metropolis draws individuals from far and wide, seeking employment opportunities or simply enjoying its offerings as visitors, whether for short or extended stays.[99]

It is interesting to compare the above wording with the introductory text in the Regional Planning of the capital area from 2001, which says under the heading: "The context of the urban landscape:"

The settlement is nestled along the coastline, sheltered by majestic mountains. Those residing in such an environment enjoy the security provided by the mountains and the expansive vistas of the open sea. The capital area's true value as a settlement lies in its unique position on headlands, embraced by towering mountains. This harmonious blend of mountains and vast coastal space allows for a distinct experience of the area within a broader context. This awe-inspiring setting holds significant weight, inspiring action and offering numerous advantages. The landscape's defining features to the north include the prominent presence of the highest peak, Esja, along with mountains, headlands, and valleys. To the south, near Garðabær and Hafnarfjörður, the lava plain takes centre stage. The diverse nature of the northern and southern regions creates distinct conditions and development opportunities. This distinction also extends to the "green scarf" that adorns the surroundings.[100]

In this setting, the romantic, rural viewpoint takes centre stage, with their primary focus on the breathtaking landscapes of mountains, headlands, valleys, the sea, and the shore. Urban landscapes, diverse human life, streets, transportation, trade and commerce, cars, bicycles, children, and buildings do not feature in their perspective. The rural essence remains ingrained in the souls of those describing the capital area. This clash of viewpoints continues to shape the ongoing discourse surrounding the city, with the notion of a car-centric urban environment embodying this mindset. The developed spaces are viewed merely as places of work or residence, with stops at shopping malls, schools, and sports facilities, and the spaces in between serving as transportation conduits. Notably, parking occupies over 20% of the public space in the city centre, with areas like Skeifan dedicating around 80% to stationary vehicles. The city boasts more than 2,000 traffic lights, equating to approximately one per 100 inhabitants.[101]

The spirit of the new zoning approach greatly differs from the outdated car-centric thinking. Collaboratively undertaken by all municipalities in the capital area, the goal is to systematically increase the usage of public transport, cycling, and pedestrian traffic by organizing the city area in a manner that makes these options viable for residents. Additionally, the aim is to establish an efficient public transport system based on the City Line (*Borgarlínan*) a Bus Rapid Transit system.

When discussing planning issues within Reykjavík and the capital area, the topic of the location of Reykjavík Airport in Vatnsmýri inevitably pops up. The airport has historically served as a central transportation hub akin to city centre train stations in other European countries, offering swift access to the city's heart upon disembarking public transport. In recent years, the location of Landspítali – The National University Hospital of Iceland, has also become entangled in this debate, as proponents of keeping the airport in place argue that it provides expedient access to the hospital for individuals who fall ill or sustain injuries outside of the city, where time is of the essence. As a result, this discussion can become emotionally charged, given the potential impact on human lives.

Nevertheless, the city authorities intend for the airport to be relocated from Vatnsmýri eventually, and significant strides have already been taken in that direction. For instance, following the ruling of the Supreme Court of Iceland, runway 06/24, often referred to as the "emergency runway" by opponents of the airport's relocation, was ordered to be closed in September 2016, based on an agreement signed between the state and the city.[102]

A rendering of the Bus Rapid Transit system Borgarlínan (City Line) pictured in front of the National Theatre on Hverfisgata, from the website of the project.

However, factors beyond Vatnsmýri's development continue to exert pressure on the airport. Domestic flights have witnessed a decline year after year, while the influx of tourists to the country has grown exponentially, highlighting an imbalance. Consequently, tourism operators across the country have begun considering the possibility of relocating domestic flights to Keflavík to provide tourists with easier access upon arrival.

Presently, everyone must pass through Reykjavík, at least for domestic flights. The same applies to rural residents needing to catch international flights. If they wish to depart from their local area by plane, they must first fly to Reykjavík Airport and then drive to Keflavík Airport, significantly prolonging their travel time.

In 2015, a committee chaired by Ragna Árnadóttir, former Minister of Justice, published a report exploring alternative locations for domestic flights, proposing Hvassahraun, south of Hafnarfjörður, as the best option for the new Reykjavík Airport.[103] The reception of this idea varied, in particular in the wake of the renewed volcanic activity on the Reykjanes peninsula since 2021, and there is still a considerable way to go before concluding the discussion surrounding Reykjavík's airport.

Regarding planning in the capital area as a whole, it is evident that significant progress has been made, shifting away from the twentieth-century mindset of an ever-expanding car-centric city towards consolidating the city and enhancing transportation options. However, this transition has not occurred without conflicts that persist. These conflicts are apparent in the differing emphases of political parties in Reykjavík. The battle lines are clearly drawn, and it will be intriguing to monitor future developments, as they will have a profound impact on city life. As of now, it is evident that the policy of the current majority will continue to prevail for the foreseeable future.

III

Reykjavík Politics

9

The Town by the Blue Channels

Reykjavík's aspiration for leadership among urban areas in Iceland is evident from the early establishment of a "city mayor" (*borgarstjóri*) in 1908, despite the town not yet meeting the criteria to be officially designated as a "city." The town council and town representatives served as the governing body at that time.

The initial elections for the Reykjavík Town Council took place in 1836, with town councillors being elected every two years. However, since 1930, councillors have held a four-year term, synchronised across all municipalities. The first elections under this new law occurred on January 26, 1930, resulting in the election of fifteen councillors in Reykjavík. Knud Zimsen was the mayor of Reykjavík when this change was implemented. Born in 1875 in Hafnarfjörður to Danish immigrant parents, Zimsen was the third Icelander to complete engineering studies. After attending Flensborg School in Hafnarfjörður, he pursued studies at Reykjavík Junior College, graduating at the young age of 17. Subsequently, he studied engineering in Copenhagen and briefly worked on sewer-related matters for the City

Engineer of Copenhagen. Driven by the emerging development opportunities in Iceland at the turn of the 20th century, Knud Zimsen returned to Iceland. He served as a municipal engineer in Reykjavík from 1902 to 1907, holding positions as a construction representative and health representative. Elected to the town council in 1908, he remained a member for ten years.

In 1914, when Páll Einarsson resigned as the first mayor of Reykjavík, Knud Zimsen applied for the position. With six years of experience as a town representative and five years as a town engineer, including a previous stint as interim mayor in 1911, Zimsen was well-placed to be appointed to the position.

In 1920, an amendment was made to the electoral law, shifting the process of electing the mayor of Reykjavík from the town council to a general election. Gunnar Thoroddsen, later a mayor and prime minister, described the election campaign between Knud Zimsen and his opponent, Sigurður Eggerz, as one of the toughest in Iceland's history. Sigurður Eggerz was no lightweight. A prominent figure in Icelandic politics, Eggerz, a lawyer, had served as a member of the Althingi, Minister of Iceland from 1914 to 1915, and Minister of Finance from 1917 to 1920. Eggerz founded the Liberal Party, which merged with the Conservative Party to form the Independence Party in 1929. He served as Prime Minister from 1922 to 1924. Despite Eggerz's notable political stature, Knud Zimsen secured the mayoral seat with a narrow margin, receiving 1760 votes compared to Eggerz's 1584.[104]

While Sigurður Eggerz later became one of the founders of the Independence Party, he had the support of Alþýðublaðið (The Social Democratic Newspaper) in the mayoral election. Knud Zimsen, on the other hand, enjoyed the endorsement of the right-wing newspaper Morgunblaðið (The Morning Paper).

On the day of the elections, May 7, 1920, Morgunblaðið's front page carried a supportive message for the mayor and, among other things, the following quote:

> *When we read Sig. Eggerz's article in Morgunblaðið the day before yesterday, a smile of pity played on our lips. - This big child, lost in the wilderness mumbles: "I have been a minister - surely I have been a minister, and I alone!"*[105]

Readers are urged to cast their votes for Knud Zimsen, highlighting his proactive and dedicated approach to his role as mayor, addressing the numerous challenges facing this young and rapidly growing township. Described as a respected individual known for his competence and strong work ethic, and for having made significant contributions.[106] In a lighthearted manner, Alþýðublaðið shares the following joke:

> *A humorous encounter took place between an elderly official in town and his acquaintance, a well-known figure in the country's political scene. The elderly official curiously inquired about his friend's choice for mayor. To which the acquaintance playfully responded, "I would vote for anyone other than Zimsen, even if they had just made a daring escape from the penitentiary!"*[107]

However, as previously mentioned, Zimsen emerged victorious in the election. In 1926, Knud Zimsen stood as the sole candidate. Following that election, the law underwent another change, granting the town council the authority to appoint the mayor, a tradition that continues to this day. In 1930, Knud

Zimsen secured his fourth term as mayor and held office during the inaugural majority rule of the Independence Party.

As noted earlier, Zimsen was not the first mayor of Reykjavík. The honour initially went to Páll Einarsson from Hraun in Fljót in the north of the country, who was elected at a town council meeting on May 7, 1908, when the choice was between him and Knud Zimsen. Zimsen received three votes at the meeting, while Einarsson received 10 votes. Einarsson served as mayor for six years and was commended for his accomplishments. Notably, various developments were undertaken in Reykjavík during his tenure, including the construction of water supply systems, gas stations, sewers, and harbours.

Knud Zimsen is buried with his wife in the Hólavalla Cemetery in central Reykjavík, where most historical figures of Iceland from the 19th and early 20th centuries are buried. Photo by the author.

Páll Einarsson assumed the position of mayor at the age of forty. He was a lawyer and had previously served as a district commissioner in Barðastrandarsýsla from 1893 to 1899. Subsequently, he was granted Kjósar and Gullbringusýsla, prompting his move to Hafnarfjörður. During his nine-year tenure as district commissioner in Hafnarfjörður, the town's population surged from 400 to approximately 1600 residents, a fourfold increase.[108]

In 1913, the newspaper *Sunnanfari* remarked that "everything [was] dead here" when Einarsson assumed office, citing the aftermath of the royal visit that had left the town in financial turmoil and heavily indebted. The royal visit pertains to King Frederik VIII's arrival in the summer of 1907. The king arrived with two ships, accompanied by warships in July of that year, causing great excitement. A website created for the 100th anniversary of home rule in 2004 provides further insight, stating:

> *To accommodate the arrival of esteemed guests, roads were paved and rivers were bridged, ensuring a smooth and convenient journey for them, with special attention given to making their luggage easily accessible. Cabins were constructed to provide accommodation, although the Icelanders themselves were content with their tents. Lavish daily feasts were organized, surpassing any previous displays of grandeur in the country. However, critics of extravagance, known as austerityists, who were a robust movement in the region, disapproved of the*

emphasis placed on wine during these celebrations.[109]

In *Sunnanfari*, Einarsson was considered to be the right man in the right place to lift the town out of this stalemate - especially by embarking on profitable job-creating projects for the community. However, the town council was hesitant about the mayor's will in these matters.[110]

Einarsson had to start by shaping the mayor's work, as the role had not existed before. Until then, the magistrates had been chairmen of the town committees- but when the town councils were established by law, they had to appoint directors. In Reykjavík, he received the title of city mayor due to Reykjavík's position as the country's capital. The mayor had to hire an "office lady," and Páll, who was then a widower, and the office lady, Sigríður Franzdóttir, fell in love and got married. Páll also bought the first typewriter in Reykjavík as far as is known. Einarsson's first son, Einar Pálsson, an engineer and professor and the first "mayor's child" in Reykjavík, i.e., a child born during a parent's term as mayor, later described his memories of tapping on the typewriter as a boy.[111]

Of course, these primitive years in Reykjavík, have been in many ways similar to what happened in new towns where European settlers were gaining a foothold, for example in North America: The construction of infrastructure. Hard-line politics of recent-arrival big-shots. Heartbreaking poverty among huge new-found riches. Although Reykjavík was a village and later a town in the Danish kingdom, it was in a way, alone. Distant. Small. But as was the case in the northern hemisphere at the beginning of the 20th century, an explosion of urbanisation was about to happen. The emigration to America that had received the "surplus people" in Iceland for several decades slowed down, and the city was taking on that role. During this period of development, there was one political force that effectively took control of the young city: The Independence Party.

10

The Long Reign of the Independence Party

The first election, where all councillors were simultaneously elected, took place on January 26, 1930, resulting in the election of fifteen councillors. A total of 11,287 votes were cast. The newly formed Independence Party, which had emerged from the merger of the Conservative Party and the Liberal Party, secured 6,033 votes, accounting for 53% of the total and resulting in the election of eight councillors. This marked the beginning of the Independence Party's majority rule in Reykjavík, which endured for an impressive 48 consecutive years until 1978. Knud Zimsen, despite serving as mayor for nearly three years since his initial term, retired due to poor health at the end of 1932.

Engineer Jón Þorláksson, the main founder and inaugural chairman of the Independence Party, assumed leadership during this time. However, his tenure was short-lived, as Pétur Halldórsson, a member of Althingi (the Icelandic Parliament) and a bookseller, took over the position in 1935. In the 1934 municipal elections, where the Independence Party retained its eight seats in the municipal council, Pétur Halldórsson had ranked eighth on the party's list.

The reign of the Independence Party coincided with the most significant period of development in Reykjavík's history. From 1930 to the party's majority loss in 1978, the population of Reykjavík nearly tripled, growing from around 30,000 inhabitants to over 80,000. It is evident that the Independence Party played a pivotal role in shaping the city's growth and development. Under their leadership, various districts such as Vogar, Hlíðar, Smáíbúðahverfið, and, notably, Breiðholt and Árbær, were planned and constructed. It goes without saying that the mayors Bjarni Benediktsson (1940-1947), Gunnar Thoroddssen (1947-1959), and Geir Hallgrímsson (1959-1972) were highly popular figures, and their aspirations extended beyond the city limits. All three later became prime ministers, with Benediktsson and Hallgrímsson also serving as chairmen of the Independence Party.

It should not be forgotten that during the party's tenure, the first woman was elected mayor, Auður Auðuns, albeit for less than a year. She served together with Geir Hallgrímsson between 19 November 1959 and 10 October 1960. She later became the first woman to serve as a government minister in Iceland. She was the Minister for Justice 1970 - 1971.[112]

The loss of the majority in 1978 came as a major shock to the Independence Party. Although the party received over 47% of the vote and needed just a few dozen votes to maintain their majority, they fell short. *Þjóðviljinn*, a left-wing newspaper, in its headline on May 30, described it as a "turning point" and suggested that the people may have been expressing discontent with both the government and the city administration. The newspaper stated, "The governing parties were routed. The workers punished the government by, in their thousands, voting for the People's Alliance. The government has received a well-deserved verdict in the local elections following successful trade union struggles in recent months."

Morgunblaðið reported, "Left-Wing Government in Reykjavík" and conducted an extensive interview with Birgir Ísleifur Gunnarsson, the outgoing mayor. Gunnarsson acknowledged the challenges faced in persuading people to vote for the IP in light of the opposition propaganda that its majority was secure.

However, the left-wing majority lasted only one term, paving the way for a new leader from the IP ranks to become the next mayor: Davíð Oddsson.

11

The City Flourishes

In 1986, exactly 200 years had passed since the village of Reykjavík was granted town rights, along with several other dry camps on this Danish island in the north. It was a significant year in Icelandic history, but it also marked the a turning point in the history of Icelandic broadcasting as the state monopoly on radio and television was broken. Stöð 2 and Bylgjan were established, bringing new soundscapes and images into the living rooms and kitchens of Icelanders. This was also a year of international victories for Iceland. The national handball team performed well at the World Cup in Switzerland, securing a 6th place finish. Additionally, Iceland boasted both Miss World, Hólmfríður Karlsdóttir, who was crowned in 1985, and the strongest man in the world, Jón Páll Sigmarsson, who claimed the title in 1986.

Reykjavík commemorated this anniversary with a splendid celebration, highlighting the new role of this old fishing village as a self-assured cosmopolitan city under the leadership of the energetic and audacious young mayor, Davíð Oddsson. Oddsson garnered nearly 53% of the vote in the municipal elections that spring, leading his party to victory. the Independence Party secured 9 out of the 15 council seats, reclaiming the power from a leaderless majority with the "independent" mayor, Egill Skúli Ingibergsson.

Davíð Oddsson (b. 1948) burst onto the political scene in 1982 like a storm. Despite his young age, he had been elected as the ninth candidate of the Independence Party to the city council in the 1974 elections. When Gunnarsson resigned and took a parliamentary seat, Oddsson became the leader of the municipal party, becoming the first minority leader of the IP in its history. In 1982, he defeated the former football hero, business tycoon and Member of Parliament, Albert Guðmundsson in a primary election for the top position and became the mayor after the party regained the majority in the spring.

Oddsson was a controversial yet immensely popular figure. The party gained support in both the 1986 and 1990 elections, with Oddsson at the helm. During his tenure, the city of Reykjavík acquired land in Grafarvogur and began developing a large district there. The city underwent a period of privatisation, reflecting the neo-liberal ideology so prevalent amongst politicians on the right during the 1980s, a new business centre was built in Kringlan where the City Theatre was relocated, Perlan in Öskjuhlíð was constructed, and last but not least, the new and magnificent town hall in the Pond (Tjörnin). The construction of the town hall faced some criticism,[113] as concerns were raised about potential damage to the lake's ecosystem. Fortunately, those concerns turned out to be unfounded.

On August 18, 1986, the 200th anniversary celebration took place. Oddson's Independence Party had received 52.7% of the vote and secured 9 city councillors in the municipal elections that very year.[114] The cake offered to the townspeople measured 200 meters long, making it the largest ever baked in Iceland. Iceland made a memorable debut on the European stage by sending its first representatives, the Icy Trio, to the Eurovision Song Contest, dressed in memorable glittering outfits. Unfortunately, their performance fell short of the nation's expectations for a grand victory, resulting in a 16th-place finish for the trio.

No event had a greater impact on the national psyche than the US-Soviet summit held at Reykjavík's Höfði Manor in October of this remarkable year. Icelanders were given ten days to prepare for the meeting, and the nation spared no effort to make it as grand as possible for Ronald Reagan and Mikhail Gorbachev, the most powerful men in the world and key figures in the Cold War. Iceland found itself in the spotlight as international media flocked to the country. Suddenly, the world's biggest names in media were gathered at Borgartún, waiting for something to happen. Days went by without any significant developments, prompting the need to entertain the people who had cast their gaze on this peculiar land, where belief in elves and trolls persisted and where the Prime Minister did not mind addressing the world press at the local swimming pool while wearing only a swimsuit. 1986 was Iceland's own version of 1989. The walls erected by the conservative politicians of the 1930s, 1940s, and 1950s around "a nation known for its literary works" crumbled with a boom. During this time, the city emerged from its hibernation of the 1970s. The streets were cleaned, most of them even paved. These were prosperous times compared to the preceding years, which were marred by societal conflicts. 1986 marked the city's coming of age as it celebrated its 200th anniversary.

Höfði Manor was built in 1909, but in 1986, it became world famous as the site of the summit between Ronald Reagan and Mikhail Gorbachev. Today, it serves as a reception centre for the City of Reykjavík. Photo by the author.

While the summit did not result in any formal agreement between the two superpowers, it is regarded as a pivotal event in the end of the Cold War. Only five years later, the Soviet Union dissolved, and most of the former Warsaw Pact countries made their way towards joining the European Union and NATO.

In 1989, Davíð Oddsson became the national deputy chairman of the Independence Party, and in 1991, he successfully ran against former Prime Minister Þorsteinn Pálsson to become the party's chairman. Shortly after, he became the Prime Minister himself in a coalition government with the Social

Democratic Party after the Independence Party achieved a significant victory in the parliamentary elections that spring. With Oddsson's departure from urban affairs to become the longest-serving Prime Minister in Iceland's history, the stronghold of the Independence Party on Reykjavík politics began to wane, and the party lost its majority in the subsequent elections and has not regained a majority in the capital since.

12

The Reykjavík List

After Davíð Oddsson's repeated election victories and decades of exclusion from the city government, the minority was ready to reconsider its tactics. Astute individuals realized that when multiple parties formed a minority against one political party, there were numerous votes that went to waste, which could be utilized by a joint candidacy to wrest majority control from the hands of the Independence Party. From 1990 to 1994, there were four parties in the minority: the People's Alliance, the Progressive Party, the Women's List, and the New Forum, which was a joint candidacy involving the People's Party and the "independent" Social Democrats. The Humanist Party and the Green Party also offered candidates in the local elections but received a combined total of 2% of the vote. In the 1990 election, the Independence Party won 60.44% of the vote and secured 10 city councilors, indicating a significant challenge for the opposition. However, opinion polls indicated that their position had weakened with the departure of Davíð Oddsson, and Markús Örn Antonsson, his successor, did not have the same presence in the city council as the current Prime Minister.

The leftists missed an opportunity to seize power; if only they had managed to unite their votes and offer a joint list, every single vote would have counted.

On Monday, January 17, 1994, an opinion poll published in the newspaper DV revealed that a joint candidacy of the minority parties, with Ingibjörg Sólrún Gísladóttir, MP for the Women's List, as the mayoral candidate, would "attract independents," as stated in the headline of the DV news article, and win 10 city representatives, while the Independence Party would secure 5.[115] The die was cast, and preparations for such a candidacy began behind the scenes. However, it required considerable skill to bring together all the adversaries within the minority parties. The Progressive Party was offered the first and sixth places on the list of joint candidates, securing their support. The People's Alliance, which regarded itself as the leading force in the minority, based on its past leadership in the city from 1978 to 1982, was offered the second and fifth places, likely resulting in two city representatives, even if a majority could not be reached. The Women's List received the mayoral candidacy in the eighth place, as well as the third and seventh places, securing a key position in the city government. The Social Democrats settled for the fourth and ninth places, as its leadership was most eager to establish this cooperation that the young Social Democrats in the city had long been advocating for. Despite the fact that New Forum had 2 city representatives and was thus the largest minority party, the Social Democrats felt they had to play the role of mediators at the table and make sacrifices for the dream of a large united leftist candidacy.

The Independents recognised that their grip on power was slipping under the leadership of Antonsson. Therefore, a decision was made to replace the mayor on March 17, 1994, just two and a half months before the election. Árni Sigfússon, a tall, eloquent young man who had received substantial support as the second candidate on the party's list behind the mayor in the party's primary election held on January 30-31 of that year, took over the reins.

The election campaign in the spring of 1994 was highly suspenseful. Only two candidates emerged, and the fight became a duel between the incumbent mayor, Árni Sigfússon, and the mayoral candidate, Ingibjörg Sólrún Gísladóttir. Most opinion polls indicated that Reykjavíkurlistinn, (The Reykjavík List), which was the name given to the joint candidacy, would emerge victorious even though the gap was closing along the way. However, a poll in the week leading up to the election predicted a victory for the Independence Party. Tension reached an unusually high level during this final week of the struggle.

Reykjavík City Hall was built into the lake in central Reykjavík during the tenure of Davíð Oddsson. It was very controversial during the time, and some believed it would kill off all life in the pond. It didn't. However, Oddsson himself never moved in. Instead, it was his arch nemesis, Ingibjörg Sólrún Gísladóttir of the Reykjavík List, who became the first mayor of the new building. Photo by the author.

In the week preceding the election, Reykjavíkurlistinn organised a large outdoor festival on Ingólfstorg, a square in the city centre. The festival commenced with a march down Laugavegur, where people gathered at Hljómskálagarður and proceeded "with trumpets and drums" to Ingólfstorg, as advertised for the event. The march drew thousands of participants, and Ingólfstorg was filled with people. Various artists performed at the festival, but when the mayoral candidate Ingibjörg Sólrún Gísladóttir took the stage as the keynote speaker, a tremendous noise started emanating from a large building at Aðalstræði 9. The house was undergoing renovation at the time, but it seemed peculiar that construction work was taking place in the house a little after 6 o'clock on a Thursday, precisely during one of the largest events held in the square. The noise was so loud that it was difficult to hear the speaker. Subsequently, a few young men from the crowd in the square entered the house and asked the workers to stop. It seemed that these construction workers had an unusual appearance and attire, although the matter was not fully investigated at the time. Nevertheless, the noise ceased, and the candidate was able to continue her speech uninterrupted. This incident briefly encapsulated the struggle that unfolded, with speculation arising as to whether the opposing party had actually orchestrated the disturbance to disrupt the gathering of their rivals.

When the votes were counted, it became evident that a turning point had occurred in Reykjavík. The left-wing coalition, led by a popular political mayor, came to power, and the Independence Party found itself in the minority for only the second time since 1930. The Reykjavík List governed the city until 2006, primarily under the leadership of Gísladóttir. She stepped down as mayor in 2003 to take on the leadership of the newly formed Social Democratic Alliance and, as Davíð Oddsson before her, enter national politics.

13

The Chaos

The decision to hire a professional mayor following Ingibjörg Sólrún Gísladóttir's departure arose due to the lack of an obvious successor within the city council group. Þórólfur Árnason, who had a background as a manager in the private sector, assumed the position on February 1, 2003. However, he quickly became entangled in a price collusion scandal involving the Icelandic oil distribution companies that were under investigation at the time, as he had previously worked as a middle manager in one of the companies. His association with the case led to his resignation after nearly two years as mayor, in order to avoid further political damage to the majority. He was succeeded by Steinunn Valdís Óskarsdóttir, a city representative since the Reykjavík List's first candidacy in 1994. Óskarsdóttir had actively advocated for left-wing cooperation and served as the first chairman of the student council on behalf of Röskva, a joint left-wing candidacy, at the University of Iceland. Her efforts played a significant role in paving the way for subsequent left-wing cooperation, such as the Reykjavík List and other joint left-wing candidacies in local councils. Like Gísladóttir, she was also involved in establishing the Social Democratic Alliance at the turn of the century.

However, there were shortcomings in the cooperation among the left-wing parties in the city. It became evident that Gísladóttir's leadership had been a vital factor in holding the parties together. When she left, the unity began to unravel. Prior to the 2006 local elections, there was no Reykjavík List. The Independence Party gained one city representative in that election, bringing their total to seven. The Progressive Party's acquisition of one city representative, Björn Ingi Hrafnsson, proved fateful. Instead of seeking cooperation with former members of the Reykjavík List, the party shifted towards the right and formed a majority with the Independence Party. After 12 years, the Independence Party, albeit in a coalition, returned to power.

As in much of the world, these were times of great prosperity in the Icelandic economy, marked by significant economic growth. The Icelandic banks had grown exponentially, their current accounts surpassing the GDP of the country itself. The city of Reykjavík possessed valuable assets, including Reykjavík Energy (*Orkuveita Reykjavíkur - OR*), which, in the spirit of the times, many wished to utilise for financial gain. The new majority established a cable company to expand OR's operations and allow private capital access to its abundant energy and human resources. Reykjavík Energy Invest (REI) was created as a subsidiary of OR, effectively serving as an "expansion arm." However, plans soon emerged to sell or merge it with the private company Geysir Green Energy (GGE), majority-owned by FL-Group, an investor, which had made substantial investments during the economic bubble years in Iceland.

This issue quickly became a political debacle, leading the Progressive Party's city representative to break from the majority. A new coalition was formed with the minority parties, and Dagur B. Eggertsson, a city councilor of the Social Democratic Alliance (Samfylking), assumed the role of mayor. A primary task of this new majority was to dismantle the expansion complex surrounding OR and terminate the merger agreement between REI and GGE, which had potentially committed the city for 20 years into the future.

The new majority consisted of councilors from the Social Democratic Alliance, the Progressive Party, the Left Greens, and a group known as Liberals and Independents. The leader of the Liberals and Independents faction was Ólafur F. Magnússon, a medical doctor who had served as a city councilor for the Independence Party for over a decade before leaving the party due to disagreements over power plant construction in East Iceland. He resigned after being labelled a "terrorist" at their national congress. Initially, Magnússon served as an independent city councilor during the 1998 election. In the 2002 local elections, he ran under the banner of the Liberals and Independents, winning re-election in 2006. Magnússon, who had been on sick leave during the formation of the new majority, returned in December 2007 and assumed the position of Chairman of the City Council. Some controversy arose when he was required to provide a medical certificate before resuming his duties, straining the cooperation. Magnússon did not fare well within the new majority, leading him to participate in its dissolution and form a new majority with the Independence Party in January 2008. The left-wing coalition had only held power for 100 days.

The loss of the majority was a significant disappointment for the left-wing parties. When Ólafur F. Magnússon assumed the mayoral position at the first city council meeting, the stands had to be cleared due to the ensuing unrest. An agreement had been reached that Magnússon would serve as mayor for one year before handing over the position to Hanna Birna Kristjánsdóttir, a councilor for the Independence Party. However, Magnússon did not complete a full year as mayor due to internal disputes within the coalition. After 203 days, the cooperation collapsed, allowing the Independence Party to form a majority with the Progressive Party once again, although Björn Ingi Hrafnsson was no longer involved.

Thus, the period from 2006 to 2010 can be described as one of the most tumultuous in the history of the Reykjavík City Council, with four different majorities and an equal number of mayors serving during that time. Additionally, the economic collapse in the autumn of 2008 diverted some of the attention away from this dramatic political spectacle. However, it was clear that a significant shake-up within the city's politics would not be unwelcome. Taking advantage of this situation, Jón Gnarr, a well-known comedian, entered the scene in autumn 2009.

14

The Best Party

There were probably not many who expected that Jón Gnarr would become the next mayor of Reykjavík when he announced his candidacy in November 2009. Gnarr openly stated that he had long desired power and a good salary, mentioning that being democratically elected was a good way to achieve that. He also expressed his desire to help his friends, as mentioned in a news release about the establishment of his party.[116] Gnarr further explained that he was forming a party and gathering people because he did not want to be alone in it "like an idiot".[117]

Gnarr's party was named the Best Party to highlight the comedic aspect of the campaign. In terms of policy, Gnarr mentioned that he had borrowed ideas from other political parties, focusing on saving homes, holding those responsible for the economic collapse accountable, and paying more attention to women, the elderly, and the poor. However, he clarified that this was just a pretext and hoped people wouldn't take it too literally, even though he admitted he might not keep his election promises.[118]

Gnarr managed to attract influential individuals to his candidate list, people who were well-known and respected for their work in various fields and had strong connections in society, especially in the cultural and creative sectors. Voters believed that despite being an artistic performance, the Best Party would be beneficial rather than detrimental to the city government. Voting for the Best Party also served as a way to express dissatisfaction with the chaos during the current election period. Nevertheless, the Best Party's significant victory came as a surprise, receiving 34.7% of the vote and securing six seats. Subsequently, the Best Party formed a majority with the Social Democratic Alliance, which had three city representatives, and one representative from the Left Greens. Jón Gnarr became the mayor of Reykjavík.

Many had anticipated that the chaos from the previous election period would continue with Gnarr in the mayor's position, but that was not the case. The cooperation between the parties went very smoothly. Dagur B. Eggertsson excelled as the chairman of the city council, and it was widely acknowledged that he primarily handled the day-to-day city politics, while Gnarr focused on other tasks associated with the office.

Today, it is evident that Jón Gnarr's candidacy for the city council was one of the most successful art projects in Icelandic history, even though its impact was felt beyond the artistic sphere. Gnarr has been described as a postmodernist artist in the role of the mayor, managing to avoid being pigeonholed as a white heterosexual man, particularly through his rhetoric, attire, and behaviour.[119] This period garnered attention from around the world and undoubtedly contributed to Iceland's strong presence in the tourism industry during the post-economic collapse years. The city had not only woken up but also become quite cool.

Gnarr stepped down after his one term as mayor to continue focusing on other aspects of his creative career. Dagur B. Eggertsson and his Social Democratic alliance took the helm. Eggertsson remained as mayor until 16 January 2024, when he stepped down for his coalition partner, and councillor for the Progressive Party, Einar Þorsteinsson.

15

The New Urbanites

In recent years, Reykjavík has experienced a noteworthy transformation driven by urban planning strategies that prioritise efficient land use within the city boundaries rather than resorting to urban sprawl. This shift in focus has significantly impacted the city's development patterns, resource utilisation, and overall sustainability.

One of the key changes brought about by this emphasis on better land use is the revitalisation of existing urban areas. Instead of expanding outward and consuming more land, Reykjavík has redirected its efforts towards redeveloping underutilised spaces within the city. Abandoned industrial zones and neglected urban pockets have been repurposed into mixed-use neighbourhoods, combining residential, commercial, and recreational spaces. This approach not only maximises land efficiency but also breathes new life into previously neglected areas, fostering a sense of community and reducing the need for long commutes.

Moreover, Reykjavík's urban planning has sought to create compact, walkable neighbourhoods that encourage active transportation and reduce dependency on cars. By strategically locating essential services, public transportation hubs, and recreational facilities in close proximity to residential areas, the city promotes a more interconnected urban fabric. This not only reduces traffic congestion and associated emissions but also contributes to a healthier and more socially engaged populace.

This has not happened in a vacuum. It has been the result of highly focussed policy changes led by the majority in the city council under the leadership of the Social Democratic Alliance and in particular, Mayor Dagur B. Eggertsson. One of his closest associates, and a leading actor in this development has been SDA Councilor Hjálmar Sveinsson.

Sveinsson, originally a journalist known for his insightful radio programs on urban matters, shared in a conversation with the author the journey that led him to his current role. His fascination with environmental issues, particularly in the context of urban living, laid the groundwork for his engagement with city planning. His radio programs delved into the intricate fabric of urban spaces, inviting conversations with architects and planners. An extended stay in Berlin, a city teeming with history and evolution, further nurtured his interest in urban environments. He began to view the city not as a mere mechanical construct but as a living organism, multi-layered and unpredictable.

While once influential, the modernist ideals of Raymond Unwin and Ebenezer Howard led to a policy shift that distanced people from urban centres, yielding adverse effects. Sveinsson challenged this notion, advocating for cities that embraced their complexity rather than trying to fit a rigid mould. His admiration for Jane Jacobs' celebration of vibrant urban coexistence influenced his perspective significantly.

The turning point arrived when he contemplated running for city council in 2010, motivated by a desire to transform his ideas into tangible actions. However, his initial stint was met with some disappointment, as, in his view, the Best Party's tenure brought forth more talk than meaningful progress. Economic challenges, including contractor bankruptcies and architect unemployment, hindered advancements. Despite these obstacles, he pressed on, contributing to projects like Miklabraut's transformation into a boulevard and the formulation of a new master plan.

Within the council, Sveinsson collaborated with like-minded individuals, including Haraldur Sigurðsson, Páll Hjaltason, Gísli Marteinn Baldursson, Kristín Soffía Jónsdóttir, and others. The group's analyses clearly depicted an escalating trend in car usage and congestion – a "predict and provide" approach that underscored the necessity for change.

A critical juncture led Sveinsson and his team to consider divergent scenarios for urban development. The two options encapsulated the stark choice between perpetuating the existing trend or promoting alternative transportation to avert gridlock. This led to a reevaluation of traditional methods in favour of environmentally-driven analyses and strategies.

Addressing the issue of urban sprawl, the city council championed a bold stance: 90% densification within existing settlement boundaries. They drew inspiration from Vancouver's remarkable transformation, emphasising the significance of fostering robust public transport networks and cycling infrastructure.

The aftermath of an economic crash allowed for a period of introspection, prompting a break of several years. While banking expansion had initially yielded deceit and manipulation, the financial crash eventually provided fertile ground for innovative change.

The prevailing ideologies in urban planning thus drive present initiatives: A shift towards an increased focus on public transport and cycling routes. The city line (Borgarlínan) concept, a Bus Rapid Transit system solidifying the vision for enhanced urban connectivity, gained momentum in Sveinson's view through diligent efforts led by the mayor, Dagur B. Eggertsson, to convince the mayors of the other municipalities in the capital area to join the initiative.

Under Mayor Dagur B. Eggertsson's leadership, a significant transformation has taken place along Laugavegur, the city's historic trading street, converting much of it into a pedestrian walkway. Photo by the author.

The conversation then pivoted to the contentious topic of the airport's relocation. Sveinsson narrated the complexities surrounding this issue, detailing the strategic manoeuvres that led to the removal of the third lane, making way for a new city district at Hlíðarendi, now almost fully built. Sveinsson underscores the importance of positioning the airport in a more strategic and viable location to accommodate the city's future growth in its most valuable area, right next to the city centre.

Discussing the significant housing predicament driven by the tourist boom and recent immigration, Sveinsson emphasised the need to avoid Soviet-style housing blocks and instead focus on thoughtful design and interstitial spaces. Efforts to build long-term rental apartments and foster collaboration with non-profit building societies were notable achievements in his eyes.

Yet, Sveinsson cautioned against the idea of boundless expansion, urging responsible urban planning and mindful growth. The challenges brought by increased immigration could be managed while preserving environmental quality and quality of life.

Sveinsson concluded with a succinct yet profound message: "Think big, start small, move fast." This American planner's maxim encapsulated the essence of Sveinsson's own journey and approach to urban transformation. The road ahead held transformative possibilities, and with an unwavering commitment, cities could evolve into vibrant, sustainable, and harmonious urban spaces.

IV

The People

16

The Reykjavíkians and Their Neighbours

When Reykjavík was being established, the Icelandic elite was not particularly fond of city dwellers or urban areas. The romantic ideology of the 19th century glorified rural life, portraying it as pure and noble. Heroes and strong-willed individuals were believed to live in connection with the land, physically fit from sports and intellectually nourished through reading. On the other hand, cities were seen as home to merchants and Jews, despised by nationalists and those embracing romantic ideals. This sentiment can be found in the writings of French, German, and English philosophers and thinkers like Jean-Jacques Rousseau, William Morris and others, as well as in Icelandic literature that praises the countryside while - despite the absence of Jews in Iceland - condemning city life. Numerous examples of this mindset exist, especially as landless people migrated to towns when the constraints of rural living loosened, with many eventually making their way to America.

During a visit to Winnipeg, where many Icelandic emigrations to the west concluded, the author discovered that Icelandic settlers had settled amongst Ukrainian immigrants in the surrounding countryside of Lake Winnipeg. While the descendants of Ukrainians still resided on farms in this region, however, the descendants of Icelanders had long since migrated "to the city" and blended into the Canadian nation.

The availability of employment in Icelandic fishing villages attracted people on a large scale, causing these villages to grow steadily at the expense of the country's rugged rural areas. The first to be significantly affected were the Hornstrandir region in the northern West Fjords. It is often humorously said that almost all city inhabitants originated from the West Fjords, as it is evident that the West Fjords have lost a considerable number of people who migrated "south" throughout the last century.

My great-grandfather, Guðmundur Sveinsson, was born in Gufunes near Reykjavík in 1870. He and his great-grandmother built a house on Hverfisgata in Reykjavík, but later moved to Frakkastígur 11, where my grandparents resided and around the middle of the last century, my parents started living together in that house too. Although my grandparents passed away when I was four years old, childhood memories of the still-standing house on Frakkastígur remain. One such memory involves my tricycle being stolen when left on the sidewalk by the steps leading up to the house. It was a great tragedy for a kid and a reminder that life in the city centre was somehow harsher than in Kópavogur, my childhood home.

The author's mother, Guðrún Sveinsdóttir, sitting on the steps in front of the house at Frakkastígur 11, probably during the Second World War. Photographer unknown.

The house on Frakkastígur is a small wooden structure with corrugated iron cladding located up the slope on the left side of the corner of Laugavegur. My mother, who grew up during the war years, recalled her childhood and teenage years there fondly. She only had to take a few steps down to Laugavegur to instantly meet someone she knew. During the 1970s, when I was a small kid, I remember being sent to buy cigarettes from a shop that, as far as I remember, was on the corner of Frakkastígur and Njálsgata. Along the way, I encountered an endless supply of chewing gum on the sidewalk in front of the convenience store, which I naturally helped myself to. Remarkably, I survived, but most of these corner shops have not.

My parents were born in the 1920s. In many ways, they were typical of their generation and the development that took place in the capital area in the years after the Second World War, as they built their home in the neighbouring municipality of Kópavogur. At this time, the development of the city largely occurred outside the administrative boundaries of Reykjavík itself, within the second and third largest municipalities in the country, Kópavogur and Hafnarfjörður. The population of Reykjavík doubled between 1920 and 1940, from almost twenty thousand to almost forty thousand. It doubled again between 1940 and 1970, reaching eighty thousand. A similar trend occurred on a smaller scale in Hafnarfjörður, which saw its population increase from about 4,000 to 10,000 during this period. Kópavogur experienced even more significant growth, with its population increasing eightfold from around 1,800 people to 14,000 between 1950 and 1980. The history of Kópavogur is closely intertwined with the history of the city, reflecting the changes in transportation and infrastructure organisation within the city area. Kringlumýrarbrautin, known as Hafnarfjarðarvegur south of Kópavogsháls and Reykjavíkurvegur when reaching Hafnarfjörður, became one of the two main transport axes in the capital, alongside Miklabraut. These main roads experience heavy traffic throughout the year. If Reykjavík were more populous, there the underground train tunnels would be. This is where Borgarlína, a Bus Rapid Transit (BRT) system, will be located once it becomes a reality.

Currently, over seventy per cent of the capital area's residents live in the suburbs and neighbouring municipalities of Reykjavík. In the districts of Reykjavík above Bústaðahverfi, more than sixty thousand people lived in 2019, which is a similar number to the city centre. When including the neighbouring municipalities, the total population in these areas is around 170 thousand out of the 245 thousand in the entire capital area. This population distribution contributes to the heavy traffic on Miklubraut and Kringlumýrarbraut, as the main business areas are concentrated in the city centre and nearby districts such as Borgartún, Suðurlandsbraut, and Múlar.

In recent years, there has been a development of lively business areas in Reykjavík's neighbouring municipalities. Heavy industry has found a place on the outskirts of Hafnarfjörður, near the aluminium smelter in Straumsvík. Trade and services have been developed in Kópavogur (Smárahverfi), which is located near the geographical centre of the capital area. Traditional industrial areas have transitioned into residential areas and shops, such as on the northern slopes of Kópavogur, Kársnes, and the centre of Hafnarfjörður.

In Reykjavík itself, slums were built in the post-war years as a result of the rapid urbanisation, similar to what happens in fast-growing cities in developing countries. People who were establishing themselves in the capital area temporarily settled in the barracks left behind by the occupation forces. Gradually, the barracks disappeared, but instead of consolidating settlements in the city centre and around the business district, the suburbs were developed. The most significant step within Reykjavík itself was the development of Breiðholt in the 1970s. Breiðholt, like many other districts in the city, derives its name from a former farm in the area. It is divided into three parts: Upper-Breiðholt, Lower-Breiðholt, and Seljahverfi.

The construction of Breiðholt was probably the most ambitious project in Reykjavík's history. It was built to address the massive housing problem in Reykjavík in the 1960s and 1970s. At that time, over two thousand people were living in unsatisfactory conditions in temporary housing. Construction began on April 6, 1967, following a declaration by the "Reconstruction Government" (as the government between 1959 and 1971 was called due to its ambitious economic program) two years earlier. The government aimed to build one thousand affordable apartments in Reykjavík for low-wage earners between 1966 and 1970. The first apartments in Lower-Breiðholt were highly sought after, with 1426 applications received for 260 apartments and 23 villas. The allocation process revealed the living conditions in Reykjavík, where it was common for adults to live in one room in their parents' houses, even with three children of their own. Many examples also emerged of couples living separately due to housing shortages.

Construction in Upper-Breiðholt began in the autumn of 1969, with the first apartments handed over a year later. The majority of the construction was completed by 1975. The district faced criticism for its high population density and perceived social segregation, as there was a disproportionately high number of single parents and individuals considered marginalized by society. These prejudices tarnished the neighbourhood's image.

Despite the initial challenges, Breiðholt became the most populous district in the city once fully built, effectively addressing many of the unacceptable living conditions that persisted in the post-war decades. The author personally experienced the neighbourhood through attending Breiðholt Junior College in the 1980s. The diversity of Efra-Breiðholt was surprising, featuring small apartments in crowded high-rise buildings, neatly designed residential areas with Swedish wooden houses, as well as large and elegant terraced and detached houses offering stunning views of the city and surrounding areas. The district provides a wide range of services, including the largest upper secondary school in the country, primary schools, sports centres, a swimming pool, football fields, shops, community centres, and other amenities, all conveniently located within the district.

In recent years, there has been an influx of immigrants to Breiðholt due to the relatively lower housing prices than in other parts of the city. People of foreign origin now comprise approximately a third of the neighbourhood's residents. This demographic shift has influenced the neighbourhood, with shops offering goods reminiscent of residents' homelands, similar to other immigrant neighbourhoods worldwide. This trend will likely increase the neighbourhood's attractiveness among the creative class, and there are indications that housing prices in Breiðholt are rising faster than in other parts of the city.

Óskar Dýrmundur Ólafsson, the district manager of Breiðholt and director of the service centre, grew up in the neighbourhood and reflects on its transformation. Although the dynamics remain somewhat unchanged, he acknowledges the changes in shape and shares a conversation he had with the poet Sjón, who is also from Breiðholt, about the old neighbourhood.

> *Oh, I remember that conversation with Sjón at Fellaskóli's birthday last year. We were just hanging out, watching the kids dance and showcase their talents. It was a fun event. At one point, I mentioned to Sjón that a lot has changed in Breiðholt, and he agreed. He said, "Yes, that's true. There are kids from everywhere here now, but in many ways, it hasn't changed that much. It was just like this when we were growing up."*
>
> *We reminisced about our childhoods and how Breiðholt used to be a place where families from all over the country and different parts of Reykjavík would come to find decent housing. It was a solution to the housing problem back then. But now, things have shifted. People are coming from all over the world to live here. It's become a diverse neighbourhood with a mix of cultures and backgrounds.*[120]

Ólafsson mentions that the same dynamic that existed in the past is still present today in Breiðholt. "The ongoing project is all about building a strong community. This is the challenge we face, and it's why we're collaborating closely with the local services of the city, forming networks and connections. Our goal is to make it easier for the community to grow, renew, and connect with one another."

Ólafsson acknowledges that when Breiðholt was first established, there were various challenges and shocks to overcome.

It took time to create the necessary conditions for people to regain stability in their lives. Although remnants of those initial difficulties may still linger in the neighbourhood's history, it's not the same situation anymore. Ólafsson adds, "Today, we are dealing with a different set of problems." Poverty and social issues have significantly decreased, but new challenges have emerged regarding multiculturalism. The focus now is on how people communicate or sometimes fail to communicate due to language barriers, cultural differences, and similar factors. "These are the issues we are actively addressing in Breiðholt."

> *You know, it's interesting how people often carry with them the experiences they had many years ago. I remember when I first arrived in the neighbourhood and had a chat with Dagur (B. Eggertsson, the mayor) and the others, saying, "Hey, we need to set the right atmosphere here, let's have a Rikkrokk (a rock festival) like back in the day." Everyone was on board, and we had these meetings where some beloved old-timers showed up. Then we had this Rikkrokk, and it was such a nostalgic gathering with all the old Breiðholt residents. However, those who currently lived there were noticeably absent. Langi Seli and Skuggarnir were playing Breiðholtsbúgí, and it was really cool, but the folks coming out of the Polish shop with their shopping bags just didn't seem interested. I guess I didn't quite read the situation well enough back then. Since then, I've been on a journey of self-discovery, trying to better understand these new dynamics and forces at play. But I still believe it's rooted in that same social capital, connections, and understanding within a community.*[121]

Nevertheless, there are clear indications that there is a darker aspect to Breiðholt. In 2016, a report released by the Icelandic Red Cross shed light on several pressing issues that were particularly prevalent in the area. A social services employee in Reykjavík emphasised in the report, "All the negative statistics reach their peak in postcode 111."[122] According to a health system expert, there is a significant amount of information that we prefer not to acknowledge regarding Efra-Breiðholt. "Low wages, widespread poverty, and a diverse mix of ethnic groups characterise the area. It appears that various social issues are prevalent within the community."[123]

In urban areas, the visible manifestations of societal inequality are often stark. The wealthiest individuals share the same sidewalks as those who endure their lives under bridges or in parks, relying on food provisions provided by volunteers and government agencies. Certain cities are teeming with people who have been left behind for various reasons, whether grappling with alcoholism, drug addiction, or severe mental disorders. Reykjavík is no exception to this. An old Icelandic term for these marginalised individuals is "rónar," which is believed to be derived from an old public house called Barón that stood on Laugavegur in the early days. It also shares similarities with the Italian word "lazarone" which was used to describe the lower class on the streets of Naples in the past. Research reveals that there is a group of homeless individuals in Reykjavík, with men constituting the majority.[124] Just over ten percent of this group live on the streets, while the majority reside in emergency shelters or unstable housing arrangements known as "unsafe housing." These individuals represent the shadowy aspects of city life. However, the inhospitable Icelandic weather ensures that the homeless population will never be very large.

Furthermore, there are those who struggle to secure safe, long-term housing for themselves and their families, even if they don't have any substance abuse issues. The housing shortage in the Reykjavík area has been intensifying in recent years. These are individuals who are unable to obtain a credit rating to purchase their own homes due to low or unstable incomes, as well as students, asylum seekers and single parents navigating the challenging rental market in the capital. The growth of tourism has further exacerbated the living conditions for this group, as many suitable housing options, such as small apartments in the city centre, have been converted into short-term rentals for tourists. This type of rental often generates significantly higher income for homeowners compared to traditional long-term rentals for families and students, albeit with added burdens.

Occasionally, there have been complaints about imbalanced construction in the city. Prior to the economic collapse, there was an extensive construction boom, resulting in a significant oversupply of new apartments. Most Icelanders are familiar with the subsequent events: the economic crash occurred, and the construction market virtually froze for years. Construction activity has gradually resumed, but many skilled craftsmen left the country after the crash, making it challenging to find workers. As a result, there has been an influx of foreign labour, particularly from European Economic Area countries. However, the trend indicates that more foreign nationals are moving to Iceland than the other way around, while more Icelandic citizens are emigrating. To some extent, this reflects the situation where the Icelandic labour market demands primarily less educated workers, leaving university-educated Icelanders struggling to find suitable employment and subsequently opting to emigrate.

If the city is to remain sustainable in the future, this situation needs to change. There are several factors working towards this goal. Reykjavík boasts a robust university that is increasingly attracting international students, who have the potential to contribute to the city's vitality by establishing businesses and working for companies that require skilled individuals in fields such as computer science and information technology. Let's turn to the topic of immigration.

17

Immigration

On 1st May 2004, ten European countries celebrated their entry into the European Union. On this historic Labour Day, Central and Eastern Europe seemed to break free, leaving behind the lingering memories of old communism and embracing the promise of capitalism in the West. Among these countries, Poland, with its substantial population, became a prominent member of the European Economic Area, which Iceland had been a part of for a decade. Young Poles wasted no time in seizing the opportunity and flocked to the lands of the West, with approximately half a million making their way to Britain.[125] In 2009, around eleven thousand Polish workers were registered in Iceland, comprising about a third of all immigrants to the country.[126] In 2022 they were roughly twenty thousand. [127] Icelanders appeared relatively positive towards these new immigrants, with surveys indicating that they held one of the most favourable attitudes in Europe when it came to welcoming immigrants into the country.[128]

One might wonder what motivates people to move across

the sea to a distant northern island in search of a better life, especially when they have a choice among all the countries of the European Economic Area (EEA), in many of which the weather can be so much more pleasant. Although the number of immigrants who arrived in Iceland during the first decade of the 21st century was relatively small compared to those who sought "high-paid" jobs in Western European countries from the new EU member states, it was still a significant number for a less populous country. Consequently, it left a noticeable impact on certain industries, particularly construction and low-skilled healthcare and tourism-related jobs.

Maltese voters celebrate outside the Prime Minister's Palace on the 9th March 2003, when it was clear the referendum on EU membership had resulted in a yes vote. Photo by the author.

Migration is a phenomenon as old as humanity itself. The

first major wave of migration occurred when mankind departed from its ancestral African homeland and gradually spread across the inhabited world. Not all waves of migration have been voluntary; the slave trade significantly altered the population composition of the New World during the early European settlement of America. In the nineteenth and early twentieth centuries, millions of Europeans and Asians migrated to America for a better life.

Until the second half of the nineteenth century, Iceland's population did not much exceed 50,000. The first census conducted in 1703 recorded a population of 50,358 in the country.[129] Various factors hindered population growth in Iceland, including famine caused by adverse weather conditions, volcanic eruptions, sea ice, and infectious diseases such as measles, smallpox, and common colds. Additionally, emigration to America occurred between 1872 and 1913, with approximately one-fifth of the population estimated to have moved during that period.[130]

Iceland was not much different from the other Nordic countries in this respect. Emigration from Norway gained momentum in the eighteenth century, followed by significant waves from Sweden during the first half of the nineteenth century. Proportionally, the highest emigration rates were observed from Ireland, followed by Norway and Sweden. Over time, Iceland reached similar levels of emigration relative to its population. Traditionally the richest economy of the Nordic countries, Denmark had the lowest emigration rates, and Finland's emigration occurred relatively late, around 1890, making it part of the Eastern European wave rather than the Nordic one.[131]

The latter half of the twentieth century was characterised by the aftermath of colonialism, during which inhabitants of former European colonies took advantage of work opportunities in their former colonial powers. The concept of "guest workers" (*Gastarbeiter* in German) also emerged in workforce-starved post-war Germany. It is important not to overlook the fact that most migration occurs within countries when people move from rural areas to cities, as was the case in Iceland throughout the twentieth century. This internal migration is particularly prevalent in developing countries, where cities have become sprawling metropolises with populations counting in the tens of millions, often characterised by unregulated slum districts and primitive living conditions.

Polish sociologist Zygmunt Bauman aptly states, "The earth is fully built," referring to the fact that uninhabited no-man's-lands, once a refuge for those displaced by modernisation and technology, no longer exist in today's society.[132] This reality has posed new challenges for economic refugees from former colonies in the global south, creating a sense that the world is overpopulated. From the perspective of globalised business and economy, fears, insecurities, and a shift towards personal security have emerged.[133]

In Iceland, the majority of immigrants have arrived legally to work, while the reception of asylum seekers was until recently less significant. It is also unlikely that there are many irregular or "illegal" immigrants, although some individuals may have entered the country unlawfully or overstayed their permitted time. The number of asylum seekers has increased significantly in recent years, in particular in the wake of the Russian invasion of Ukraine in 2022.[134]

What impact does this type of immigration have on nations and societies? Recent studies indicate that immigrants have a positive impact on national economies, and there is no reason to believe that Iceland is an exception to this trend.[135] Contrary to popular belief, other studies show that immigrants have little effect on the employment or unemployment rates of native-born individuals, as they often fill jobs that locals are unwilling to take. Those most affected by competition from immigrants are those with lower levels of education and social status. Furthermore, immigration does not lead to a decrease in wages, as commonly claimed, and immigrants do not burden the welfare system. As healthy, working-age individuals who have come to work, they become net taxpayers from the outset.[136]

The societal impact of this type of immigration varies significantly between regions and even districts. Immigrants tend to concentrate in specific areas, forming social support networks, a pattern observed not only in Iceland but also elsewhere.

18

Double Residency

Naturally, we all have a connection to the places where we have lived or had enjoyable experiences. It could be the neighbourhood we grew up in, went to school, or played in as children. It could be the countryside town where we spent time or the village where we made memories during a summer of young love. These emotional connections to places are a common human tendency. Therefore, Icelanders who have lived abroad for a while are likely to return home because "there is something about this country, despite the wind and horizontal rain." In previous centuries, there were rumours that Icelanders were unsuitable for the Danish navy because they would feel homesick as soon as the ship left the shores of Iceland.

The concept of "place" is significant in urban studies and the sociology of cities. Sociologists Anthony M. Orum and Xiangming Chen[137] argue that "place" plays a central role in our lives, as it defines our identity. While technological advances have reduced the importance of physical space, it remains an integral part of our lives. Whether it's a hotel room, conference room, or family home, we are always in a place where human behavior occurs. Orum and Chen identify four connections that bind us to specific places:

Firstly, our sense of individuality or self. Every person experiences a connection between themselves and the places they have lived. They may form emotional attachments to houses that are to be demolished or neighbourhoods that are undergoing change. They fight against these changes because they perceive these places as part of themselves and their lives.

Secondly, our sense of community and belonging. Urban districts are not just spaces where people interact; they also become communities connected to a particular place. Examples like Breiðholt in Iceland demonstrate how neighbourhoods can hold symbolic value and foster a sense of identity among their residents.

The third connection is our sense of the past and the future. Immigrant districts exemplify this connection. Immigrants often believe that moving to a new place in a new country will bring them more happiness and success than their place of origin. The new place becomes a symbol of a better life, and the past becomes a distant place associated with memories and emotions. This connection reflects the belief that we have moved forward, leaving the past behind.

The fourth connection is the feeling of being at home and comfortable in a place. This feeling strengthens the previous connections. Feeling out of place is unpleasant and being in the right place contributes to our well-being. For Icelanders, hearing "Welcome home" upon landing at Keflavík Airport fills them with a sense of well-being.

In recent decades, it has become increasingly common for

people to have homes and connections in two cities, often in different countries. German architect and urban planner Bernd Upmeyer has studied this tendency among Germans of Turkish descent. Whether they moved to Germany from Turkey in the 1960s and 1970s as part of the labour force during the German economic post-war boom, or their children and grandchildren, they often maintain relationships and social connections in both cities simultaneously. This phenomenon challenges prevailing notions of identity and cultural roots. It is a sociological phenomenon that transcends class distinctions and affects individuals from various backgrounds.[138]

This complex situation further complicates the understanding of identity and cultural belonging. Individuals living in two places simultaneously experience a sense of longing and desire, where their "at home" becomes a "non-place" and a utopia. They long for the familiar aspects of their Turkish city, such as the chaos, family ties, good weather, and grandmother's food when they are in Germany. Conversely, they long for the order, clean public transport, respect for traffic rules, friends, colleagues, and even the bad weather when they are in Turkey.

Reykjavík also hosts a group of individuals who have a connection to the city as a place to work and raise their children while still maintaining a hometown in another country where their family and childhood friends reside. This likely applies to a large group of immigrants who have settled in Reykjavík over the past two decades. In 2019, immigrants accounted for 19% of Reykjavík's population, compared to 2.9% in 1998. The distribution of immigrants across districts varies, with Efra Breiðholt having over a third of its population composed of immigrants.[139]

There are also those who were born and raised in Reykjavík

but have moved to other countries, especially in the aftermath of the economic crisis in 2008-9. Their connections to the city and other cities, and the role Reykjavík plays in their identities, raise interesting questions. How do immigrants experience living in the world's northernmost capital? How do they navigate their ties to their hometowns?

In recent years, extensive research has been conducted on the experiences of immigrants and cross-border mobility. These studies aim to understand the causes, consequences, and economic impact of this phenomenon on the countries involved. Attention has also been given to how this impacts the diversity of self-identities and the cultural symbols that characterise the life experiences of diaspora groups. It is particularly intriguing to consider the concept of cognitive dissonance, where individuals must choose between two favourable options, highlighting the existence of incompatible subjective activities, thoughts, perceptions, opinions, attitudes, desires, and intentions within each person.

This discussion is related to theories of nationalism, such as Benedict Anderson's concept of "imagined communities." Anderson argues that social consciousness can be created without physical contact with a specific place or community. He introduces the term "long-distance nationalism" in this context.[140] An example of this is the participation of Turks living abroad in a referendum held by Turkish President Recep Tayyip Erdogan to increase his power. Turkish immigrants in Germany, for instance, have shown greater support for increased Turkish nationalism compared to those residing in Turkey.

Communication expert David Morley suggests that this long-distance nationalism is evident in the satellite dishes found in the suburbs of Paris, owned by North African immigrants. These satellite dishes, known as "antennes parabolique," have attracted attention and have been perceived as hindering the integration of immigrants into French society. However, sociologist Kevin Robins, who has studied Turkish immigrants in London, refutes this claim, stating that these satellite dishes are not central to the lives of these individuals. Instead, they help immigrants navigate between multiple worlds and create a new self-image that aligns with their current reality, oscillating between virtual existence and the physical reality they find themselves in.

Cultural scientist Regina Bittner argues that these new realities found in immigrant districts, such as Rosengård in Malmö, Kreuzberg in Berlin, and Hoogvliet in Rotterdam, can no longer be described solely in reference to their country of origin or the new country. These neighbourhoods often derive their vibrancy and international character from the informal and family-oriented economic activities of immigrants. They also attract the creative class, as described by Richard Florida in his book "The Rise of the Creative Class," which highlights how the creative class drives the fate of urban communities through their choice of location. These communities thrive in diverse, liberal, and open-minded environments. Florida asserts that "creativity" has become a more significant factor than "capital" and "labour" in determining economic success.[141]

According to Gallup surveys conducted worldwide on people's willingness to relocate, it is noteworthy that Iceland ranks high on the list when considering its population size (per capita). In fact, Iceland ranks third in the world (preceded only by New Zealand and Singapore). If all those who expressed interest in moving to Iceland were given the opportunity to do so, the country's population would increase by 208%. If only looking at young people, or people between the ages 15-29, Iceland tops the list and would see that age group increase by 451% if all who wished to move to Iceland were allowed to.[142] While it is highly unlikely for such a scenario to occur, targeted measures could attract a fraction of this number to the country. These measures might include expanding the availability of higher education in English, as previously mentioned, or implementing immigration policies similar to those adopted by Canada.

19

A Promised Land

In recent centuries, we have witnessed examples of societies primarily or entirely built on immigration. Many of these societies are among the wealthiest and most prosperous in the world. Canada, New Zealand, Australia, and the United States, of course, are prominent examples. However, there are also immigrant countries that have faced challenges and achieved lesser success, such as certain Latin American ones. Several studies have explored the reasons behind this disparity, citing factors like culture, religion, racism, colonial heritage, institutions, climate, and distance from affluent markets.

Knowing that immigration to Iceland has been sharply increasing, and from the Gallup poll mentioned in the previous chapter, it could increase even further, let's consider what kind of immigrant country Iceland could become. It is crucial to acknowledge the obstacles that need to be overcome for Iceland to succeed as such a nation. Firstly, the country's legal framework is more focused on restricting immigration, except for its membership in the European Economic Area (EEA), which allows for free movement between European countries.

The fact is that most EEA countries do not possess individuals who are prepared to face the linguistic and climatic challenges prevalent in Icelandic society. However, many individuals from economically, politically, and socially disadvantaged countries outside the European Union are willing to tackle these barriers. This opens the possibility for immigrants from regions like South-Asia, China, Latin America, the Middle East, and Africa to come to Iceland.

Between 1872 and 1913, a fifth of the Icelandic population emigrated to North America, many finding their way to Gimli, Manitoba, where this picture of the author was taken in 2002. The sign says "Jökulsá" an Icelandic word for a glacial river. Despite Lake Winnipeg being frozen solid at the time and looking not much different than a glacier, a river was nowhere to be found. In the distance, a statue of a horned Viking can be seen, celebrating the Nordic heritage of the townspeople. Photo by Runólfur Ágústsson.

If Iceland were to open up to immigration beyond the EEA, it is likely that most immigrants would settle in Reykjavík. We would witness a similar pattern of development in the city as seen in other immigrant cities like San Francisco and Seattle in the United States, as well as Vancouver in Canada. Initially, immigrants tend to congregate in specific districts, such as Chinatown and the Mission in San Francisco. The latter primarily houses Mexican immigrants, where Spanish is spoken in the streets, Catholic churches adorn the squares, and the climate is hotter due to geographical factors, evoking a sense of Mexico. The same applies to Chinatown, characterised by Chinese signage, Asian passers-by, and the aroma of sweet and sour sauce and grilled meat permeating the air. San Francisco also has subsequent stages in the development of such neighbourhoods, including an Italian neighbourhood. That neighbourhood still flies Italian flags on balconies, and the proportion of pizza places is suspiciously high. However, there is a trend typical of such neighbourhoods, where the second or third generation of immigrants move away once they have gained education and assimilated into the country's existing customs, blending into the broader society.

Canada has long been at the forefront of Western immigration policy.[143] It is experiencing a higher influx of economic immigrants than the total population of Iceland each year. The stated goal of Canadians is to manage immigration by actively integrating immigrants into society, considering that Canada itself was built by immigrants, initially from France and the UK, and later from various countries in Northern and Eastern Europe.[144] The active integration process involves several steps. Firstly, the Canadian government selects immigrants and refugees allowed to enter the country through its embassies and other foreign service activities. Secondly, immigrants are placed in specific locations and provided support through the system during their initial years of residence. The third step is the acquisition of Canadian citizenship and long-term integration into society. The objective is for all immigrants to become fully participating members of Canada in economic, social, cultural, and political aspects.[145]

When selecting immigrants, Canada considers three main categories: economic factors, family ties, and refugees. Economic immigrants are selected based on their potential to contribute to the labour market, taking into account factors such as education, skills, work experience, and proficiency in English or French. Family-based selection involves spouses, children, and close relatives of other immigrants. Refugees are selected based on the threats they face in their home countries, and they are more likely to have health issues, limited education, or lack language skills relevant to the Canadian labour market.

The estimated transition period to Canadian society is approximately five years, during which immigrants are offered various free services such as job search assistance, language learning programs, and support in building social connections. The final stage of this transition period, as mentioned earlier, is the acquisition of Canadian citizenship.[146]

Overall, immigration policy in Canada is considered successful, particularly in terms of social integration. The majority of immigrants express a strong sense of belonging and satisfaction with their lives in Canada, as shown in opinion polls. The positive outcomes can be attributed to the mutual adjustment between immigrants and society. Immigrant integration involves federal, provincial, and local governments, community service providers, educational institutions, trade unions, employers, and individuals. In international comparisons, Canada ranks highly, particularly in anti-discrimination measures according to the Migrant Integration Policy Index (MIPEX), and it is known for having the most positive attitude towards immigrants among OECD countries.[147]

Anne-Tamara Lorre, a former Canadian Ambassador to Iceland, has a fascinating personal history. She moved to Canada from her native France as an adult to attend university and became fascinated with Canadian society. She settled in Canada, became a citizen, and eventually became one of the country's ambassadors. Lorre believed that as a woman, she had better opportunities for advancement based on merit in Canada compared to the more traditional and conservative society she perceived in France.[148]

Lorre believes that Iceland, as a relatively young society in terms of large-scale immigration, has the potential to develop better immigration policies compared to larger European countries like France and Germany. In France, there is considerable hostility towards immigrants, and they often feel marginalised by the policies implemented there. On the other hand, Canada places a strong emphasis on community participation and actively encourages Canadians to welcome and integrate immigrants into society. It is important to note that while there is some opposition to immigrants in Canada, many new immigrants have achieved great success, and even first-generation immigrants hold positions as Members of Parliament and ministers.[149]

Since 1990, Canada has received over six million immigrants.[150] Although this number may not appear significant in a country with a population of 35 million, considering that immigrants and their descendants likely make up over 20% of

Canada's population, it demonstrates the impact of immigration. The distribution of immigrants varies across the country, with the highest concentrations found in major cities such as Toronto, where 52% of the population was born outside Canada in 2011, and approximately 40% in Vancouver.[151] Despite the challenging climate and long, dark, and cold winters, Canada consistently ranks among the top countries for quality of life.

If Iceland were to adopt immigration laws similar to Canada, including a points-based system based on education, work experience, and language proficiency, it would likely result in a partly English-speaking Iceland. In fact, scholars at the University of Iceland state that, as of today, English can no longer be regarded as a foreign language in Iceland. Formally accepting that would be a significant step for a country that places importance on preserving its "old" language. It would be a challenging endeavour, and it might be more realistic to consider countries other than English-speaking nations for language considerations.

Israel has been one of the largest recipients of immigrants in recent decades. Since its establishment in 1948, over 3 million individuals have immigrated to Israel. The largest group, approximately 1.2 million people, came from the former Soviet Union, particularly after its collapse in 1990.[152] Israel's immigration policy is based on unique principles, mainly granting entry to individuals who can demonstrate their Jewish heritage. Upon arrival, they are granted Israeli citizenship. Israel has also revived Hebrew as a living language, albeit not the same language as the ancient biblical texts. The Hebrew spoken in Israel is in fact a new language which could just as well be called "Israeli". New residents in Israel put significant effort into learning Hebrew, and extensive courses called "ulpan" are conducted to facilitate their language acquisition. Hebrew is the dominant language in the country, alongside Arabic, which is the mother tongue of a significant portion of the population. New residents are encouraged to learn the local language, which has its own alphabet.

Therefore, there is no indication that with substantial investment, it would be impossible to maintain Icelandic as the language of the people, even with a significant increase in immigration. However, due to the proximity and extensive communication with the English-speaking world, it is likely that English will gradually gain more prominence in Iceland, similar to what has happened on another island in the North Atlantic Ocean, Ireland.

20

Destination Reykjavík

How do the new inhabitants feel in this northern city where darkness reigns for half the year and endless daylight dominates the other half? According to research conducted by MIRRA, the Centre for Immigrant Research, many people work long hours. Examining their origins reveals that the majority are of European descent, have light skin, and follow the Christian faith. Approximately half of them come from Poland.[153]

The Red Cross in Reykjavík recently prepared a report on disadvantaged individuals in the city, with a particular focus on immigrant children. The report highlights a genuine risk of social isolation for these children. While the city has various initiatives in place to address these issues, such as youth workshops and after-school programs, there are still challenges.[154] "They feel lost and disconnected – primarily due to language difficulties. They lack proficiency in their native language and therefore struggle with learning Icelandic," states the report.[155]

According to a 2023 survey by the Icelandic Confederation of Labour (ASÍ), almost 37% of respondents suffered a rights violation/violations in the labour market recently in the preceding 12 months. However, relatively more immigrants have suffered these offences, or 56% of immigrants. A third states various violations on account of their skin colour.[156]

Although Poles and other Europeans form the largest immigrant group in Reykjavík, it is possible to find individuals from diverse backgrounds. Among those born outside of Europe, aside from those born in the United States, Thais and Filipinos constitute the largest non-European groups in Iceland. However, these individuals are primarily "legal" immigrants who have arrived through marriage or family reunification. Iceland has traditionally been relatively less open to asylum seekers due to its geographical position, as it is not typically the initial entry point for asylum seekers in the Schengen area.

However, since the Russian invasion of Ukraine, this figure has quadrupled annually, with around half of the asylum seekers from Ukraine, (seekers from Ukraine are automatically granted permission to stay), and much of the rest from Venezuela and Palestine, although some also from Iraq, Nigeria, Syria, Somalia, Afghanistan, and Iraq. Following the so-called Dublin Regulation, within Schengen, those who have earlier been granted asylum in another Schengen country are almost always sent back there.

So, how does Reykjavík welcome new residents from abroad? Reykjavík is part of the Intercultural Cities network, which assesses how well cities address the challenges of multiculturalism and immigration. Various service aspects are systematically evaluated, and the interactions between new residents and the city are rated. Subsequently, a report is published with recommendations and examples from other cities that can serve as inspiration. Out of the 127 cities that have undergone this assessment, Reykjavík ranks 50th with a score of 64% on the aggregate intercultural city index. This is the same score as Logrono in Spain and Sherbrooke in Canada. Reykjavík falls between Erlangen in Germany (63%) and Rubicone in Italy (65%). Additionally, Reykjavík ranks 18th among cities with fewer than 200,000 inhabitants.[157] This is a significant change in a short time, since in 2014, Reykjavík scored only 37% on this index.[158]

According to Anna Kristinsdóttir, the director of human rights in the city of Reykjavík, there is anyhow room for improvement. She notes that since 2008, the city's efforts have primarily focused on coordinating the services provided. "As a municipality and as the capital, we often find ourselves providing services that should not be our responsibility. We are now trying to prioritise this issue by ceasing our own services and involving the relevant stakeholders in this project."[159]

She identifies the lack of knowledge among staff as the primary challenge within the city's system. She explains, "When we encounter a large number of people who speak different languages and belong to different cultures, the systems and consequently the staff, although we have about 8,000 employees here in the City of Reykjavík, sometimes face difficulties."[160] Anna emphasises that there is not always a willingness to help these individuals, stating, "Some people believe that these individuals are taking something away from us that we should have for ourselves." She adds, "Our main task has been to educate employees, which we find to be the most demanding aspect, and to demonstrate that Icelandic society needs these people." Anna argues that Icelandic society benefits from immigrants and presents the following arguments to support her claim.

> *It is crucial to consider who will provide care for individuals entering nursing homes. Based on statistics from Statistics Iceland, it is evident that when we examine population trends for the next 20 to 40 years, the sustainability of society and its ability to maintain existing services and activities will be greatly compromised without significant migration from abroad. We require greater diversity. Our nation has been predominantly homogeneous for an extended period, and it is evident that as soon as we welcome diverse groups of individuals from foreign origins, our city and culture undergo a significant transformation. This diversity enriches our society, education, and overall identity, embodying the essence of a vibrant and sustainable community. Having resided in this city my entire life, I have witnessed the tremendous contributions these individuals from around the world bring to us.*[161]

But how do the new Reykjavikians themselves describe the city? Why did they move here, and how does it compare to their previous residence? To get a small insight into that, I spoke to a few of them, mostly young, creative people from Poland and other European countries, but also some from further afield. To my surprise, the weather did not seem to bother them at all. Some described it as wonderful.

José Luis Anderson (28) from Mexico is a musician. He says he loves the weather in Reykjavík. "Contrary to expectations, it wasn't unbearably cold. People often assume that because Iceland is close to the North Pole, it must always be freezing.

However, I knew that the average temperature rarely drops below -15°C in the coldest months. What I didn't fully anticipate was the wind, which could be even more challenging than the cold itself. Despite that, I was enchanted by the snow. I hadn't experienced living in a city blanketed in snow before, and it felt like living in a winter wonderland. I'm a romantic at heart, and to me, it was pure poetry. I took inspiration from it to write and create."

Marysia (Maria Zofia Tyszkiewicz) is 29 from Poland. She works in a bar and loves the Reykjavík weather as well. "I actually love it! The ever-changing and unpredictable Icelandic weather is a source of fascination for me. I find the intensity of the weather and the connection to nature invigorating. It keeps me feeling alive." Klaudia Karolina Kaczmarek (32) is a sculptor from Poland. She agrees, "I actually love the weather here in Iceland. It's refreshing to live in a place where you can feel the wind and experience the elements."

Lara de Stefano (37) is from Italy and operates a business importing electric cars. She finds the winters challenging but loves the summer. "I love the Icelandic summers because they're not too hot, unlike in Italy, where it can be scorching. Here, I can enjoy the pleasant weather and the long daylight hours without feeling overwhelmed by the heat."

Lolo (Lorenz Brunnert) is 30 years old from Germany and has worked as a farmhand. He enjoys the Icelandic weather. "I actually appreciate the cold and darkness here, finding solace in creating a warm, cosy environment indoors. The weather has even shaped some of my experiences, like searching for sheep in a snowstorm. It's made me resilient."

Silvia Raitschev (40) from Germany says the weather in Reykjavík can be annoying at times, "but it doesn't upset me. I chose to live here, and having good heating and not having to worry much about heating costs is a luxury." She also appreciates the natural hot water and the opportunity to go to the swimming pools. "It's a different lifestyle." Silvia is currently working in Malawi for the Icelandic Red Cross, but she intends to return to Iceland when her mission concludes.

But what drew them to Reykjavík? Most mention the closeness to nature. "I love the nature, the freedom, and the small yet vibrant city of Reykjavik. It offers a unique combination of being close to nature while still having the advantages of a capital city," says Marysia, and continues: "In Reykjavik, it feels like you can truly be yourself without judgment. Your occupation doesn't define you, and you can explore your passions and creativity freely. This sense of freedom is a stark contrast to some other places, including Poland, where life can be more challenging." Lara says: "Well, besides the magic and folklore, I was also interested in the culture and nature of Iceland. I wanted to explore the unique culture here, experience the Northern Lights, and be close to nature. The economic aspects, like the economic crisis and tourism, also piqued my interest." Klaudia says the landscape is breathtaking, "with mountains covered in snow even during the summer. When I hear the ocean and see the snow-covered mountains, it brings a warm feeling to my heart. I appreciate being so close to nature and feeling connected to the earth."

Marta Staworowska (38) from Poland works as a goldsmith and is a bit of an adventurer. Before she moved to Iceland, she was in the Polish Army and served in Afghanistan for a while. She says: "Well, speaking from my perspective within my own social circle, it appears that the people here exude positivity, embrace artistic expressions, enjoy traditions, savour coffees and hot chocolate, marvel at the auroras, appreciate leisurely walks, and frequent vibrant shops. They form a distinct community, and living in Iceland is no walk in the park; it's not as easygoing as, say, Spain. You truly need something profound that resonates with your heart to choose Iceland as your home. Personally, I have come to the realisation that Reykjavik is a fantastic choice, and it's my preferred place. I have no intentions of considering a change."

Klaudia Karolina Kaczmarek works as a sculptor and enjoys the Icelandic weather. Here she is dressed in a traditional Icelandic sweater, Lopapeysa, at the Diamond Beach. Photo by Tytus Łataś

José says he didn't choose Reykjavík per se. "Well, initially, I didn't exactly choose Reykjavík. At the outset, my goal was to study for a master's degree abroad. So, I started looking for programs that aligned with my interest in music. I found options in both Iceland and Ireland, applied to both, and was accepted by both. Iceland seemed more promising regarding the cost of living, and I had never been to Iceland before. There was a strong, almost intuitive pull toward Iceland. So, I decided to trust my gut feeling and make the journey."

When asked about how it is integrating into Icelandic society and whether they have been met with any prejudice by the locals, their answers vary. Silvia, who speaks fluent Icelandic, says she has not found it easy to integrate into Icelandic society. "This is something I've heard from many other foreigners as well. It has been a challenge to build strong connections and friendships with Icelandic people. The initial openness often wanes, and people become less committed to building relationships."

Marta says that she has Icelandic friends. "But my connection with the Polish community is exceptionally strong. I was somewhat concerned initially that the Icelandic people might not be entirely welcoming towards us. However, I believe it's actually a significant positive for them because it adds diversity to Iceland. With people from all corners of the world, they seem to be quite content with the variety it brings."

Lolo says he has been fortunate. "Learning the language and immersing myself in Icelandic culture helped me integrate smoothly. However, I recognise that some of my friends have faced discrimination."

Silvia says she has definitely encountered prejudices. "Having a Bulgarian name, I believe that many of my job applications were not properly considered. In a job interview, the manager expressed surprise that I spoke Icelandic well as if it were unexpected." Silvia mentions that she also implied that she must not have written her application herself, since it was error-free.

Most of them mention that sometimes it irritates locals not being able to communicate in Icelandic. Lara mentions that at university, there were instances where she wanted to join groups for projects with Icelandic students, "but I was told that they preferred to work only with each other. This made me feel like an outsider".

Klaudia hasn't had difficulties in making Icelandic friends. " One noticeable difference is the Icelandic sense of humour, which I find to be quite unique and enjoyable. People here are generally more relaxed and easygoing, especially when compared to the busyness and sometimes seriousness of life in Poland. There's also a strong sense of community among those who have moved to Iceland, and it's a welcoming and supportive atmosphere." Marysia agrees. "While I don't have extremely close Icelandic friends, I do have acquaintances and people I interact with. Language barriers can sometimes limit closer friendships, but I'm working on learning Icelandic."

José says that one of the things he noticed was the contrast in how social interactions happen in Iceland compared to his previous experiences back home in Mexico. "Initially, I was eager to reach out and connect with people. However, I found that Icelanders can be more reserved in their interactions, especially in daily life when sober."

Lolo says he has a close circle of German friends here; however, over time, some of them have moved away. "People frequently come and go in this place. While my connections are diverse, there's a noticeable presence of individuals from Poland here, shaping a significant portion of the community."

The Polish interviewees all mention the strong Polish community in Iceland. "We're often jokingly referred to as the "Polish Mafia", Marta says. "The community is incredibly supportive, helping newcomers settle in and navigate life here."

Other challenges mentioned are the situation in the housing market, where it can be difficult to find housing, and it is quite expensive when found, and the lack of adequate public transportation and cycling infrastructure. Silvia says: "I grew up on the outskirts of Berlin. Living in Reykjavík is quite different, mainly regarding public transportation and the ability to cycle. The cycling infrastructure needs improvement. It's a bit frustrating that lessons haven't been learned from other European cities." Klaudia mentions the bus system, "It's not so much about how it operates but more about the ticketing system. The one-hour tickets make it more economical for people to use their cars instead of the bus, which leads to more traffic congestion."

Lara says she has noticed that the housing market in Reykjavík, whether for buying or renting, can be quite expensive. "It's not limited to downtown Reykjavík; it's a widespread issue. The prices seem to keep rising, and it's challenging for many people, especially those who are looking to buy their first home."

Asked whether they plan to stay, most of them do. "Reykjavík feels like home now, and I'm not thinking of going back any time soon," says Silvia. Lara says she wants to build her future here. "Italy, like many other places, has its issues, and I see a brighter future for myself here in Iceland." Klaudia says she hopes to stay in Iceland. "However, it's currently a bit challenging because my apartment contract is uncertain due to some unique circumstances. We'll have to see how that situation unfolds, but I'm optimistic about my future here." Marysia says she plans to stay in Iceland indefinitely. "I feel at home here and appreciate the opportunities and lifestyle it offers." Lolo says he envisions staying another eight to ten years, "especially for my daughter's sake. However, I'm open to new opportunities elsewhere if life takes me there. For now, Reykjavik feels like home, and I'm in no rush to leave."

José says his life is now deeply rooted in Reykjavik. "I've built a strong community here, both personally and professionally. My network, my job, my studio, and my fiancé are here. The only thing missing is my parents. So, unless immigration authorities decide otherwise, I plan to stay in Reykjavik for good. My commitment to contributing positively to Icelandic society is unwavering."

21

A Clash of Cultures

For the last two decades or so, during the second weekend of August, two well-attended festivals have taken place in Iceland, both focused on friendship and charity. The Gay Pride Days gather LGBTQ+, their friends, and supporters in Reykjavík to celebrate diversity. Since its inception in 1999, the festival has steadily expanded, now lasting several days filled with vibrant colours and festivities. Approximately seventy thousand people participate in the festival's events in the city centre, particularly the procession held on Saturdays.[162] Notably, during Jón Gnarr's mayoral term (2010-2014), his active involvement in the festival garnered special attention. He would dress in drag and ride on one of the creatively decorated floats, even causing controversy in Russia one year by depicting a member of the Pussy Riot punk band, previously mentioned in this book, in a different context. There have been discussions that the Reykjavík procession has grown larger than June 17, the National Day of Iceland, which has long been Iceland's most prominent national festival.

During the same weekend in August, in the town of Dalvík,

enterprising individuals, aided by generous sponsors, serve fish dishes on the town's streets. In 2014, an estimated 26,000 to 28,000 people attended the festival,[163] and the number steadily increased since its inaugural celebration in 2000.[164] Icelanders flock to Dalvík in large numbers, arriving in their pick-up trucks with caravans in tow, to relish in good food, drinks, and the company of family, friends, and fellow festival-goers. It can be viewed as a delightful contrast: the multicultural city celebrating diversity without direct reference to Icelandic culture and heritage, juxtaposed with a festival where the "basic industry" takes centre stage.

To categorise these two festivals as representatives of opposing currents in Icelandic society is a considerable oversimplification. While Gay Pride undoubtedly represents the pinnacle of liberal ideas and ideals of equality for all, regardless of sexuality or other characteristics, Fish Day does not necessarily embody the opposite: conservatism. Nevertheless, Fish Day serves as a display of national heritage, honouring the lifeline provided by the high seas. It highlights Icelanders' struggle against the forces of nature and the rewards they enjoy, sitting on the grass in front of their caravans with a beer in hand.

These two festivals bear similarities to events found throughout the Western world. In the United States, for example, city parades such as those in San Francisco and Seattle, alongside barbecues and rodeos in Texas, reflect the cultural diversity found in melting pots, while also celebrating deep-rooted national cultural heritage in its most popular manifestation. These two currents have increasingly taken on political dimensions, i.e., the "nationalism" and "internationalism" axis, in addition to the more traditional "capitalism" and "socialism".

The longstanding urban-rural divide serves as another divisive axis in politics, strongly influencing attitudes toward issues such as immigration and European Union membership. This division is not unique to Iceland and has been evident in referendums on Norway's EU membership in 1972 and 1994[165] as well as the Brexit referendum in 2016, highlighting the divide.[166]

As previously mentioned, living in Iceland would likely be affected if a vibrant, dynamic, and fairly populated city had not developed, offering most, if not all, the amenities that cities of a similar size have to offer. Iceland has resisted the trend seen in neighbouring countries like Greenland and the Faroe Islands, where individuals seeking modern comforts have migrated out of the country to places like Copenhagen, where their skills, ideas, and creativity find better outlets.

At the same time, Reykjavík has long portrayed an image that, in many ways, diverges from Icelandic national culture, thus being actively in opposition to the forces aiming to create an Icelandic nation. However, it is essential to recognise that this is not an exclusively Icelandic phenomenon. Cities have long been targets for those seeking to uphold conservative values, including individuals who, by the standards of their time, could be considered liberal, such as Jean-Jacques Rousseau and Thomas Jefferson.[167] These conflicts manifest in various ways, some overt and direct, such as direct opposition to urban development, while others are more concealed and indirect. An example of the latter could be the struggle for Reykjavík Airport in Vatnsmýri, which, according to Reykjavík authorities, has long hindered the city's growth and progress.

On June 17, 2014, the national holiday festival was, as usual, inaugurated at Austurvöllur in front of the Parliament, featuring an address by the Prime Minister at the time, Sigmundur

Davíð Gunnlaugsson of the Progressive Party, along with musical performances. Interestingly, a choir from Skagafjörður in the north of the country was chosen to sing the national anthem at the festival, marking the first time that a choir from the countryside was hired for this occasion in this location. Reports in the media indicated that this decision incurred some expenses to be covered by the Prime Minister's Office.[168] Speculations arose that these celebrations had become somewhat stagnant, leading social critic Illugi Jökulsson to comment on his Facebook page:

> *Listen, it is crucial for me to exercise caution now and ensure that I am not wrongly accused of being unpatriotic under any circumstances. That is not something we desire. However, take a moment to consider this. The ceremony at Austurvöllur raises some intriguing points. Scouts are standing as the guard of honor. Scouts? Are scouts even a thing anymore? And why do the young ones give a salute resembling soldiers? Furthermore, why is there a brass band dressed in costumes from the early 20th century? From a visual standpoint, this spectacle could very well be transplanted from 1944. Isn't there room for some graphical updates? Must it look EXACTLY as it did 70 years ago? Would it be sacrilegious to wear slightly more contemporary attire or perform newer music? Is this ceremony preserved in a 70-year-old formaldehyde, encapsulating the essence of the "Republic of Iceland"?*[169]

Jökulsson continues his critique, focusing on the attire of the Reykjavík Trumpet Band. He remarks, "The costumes of the trumpet band resemble those of a destitute village in a mountain valley in the Austro-Hungarian Empire in 1914. Why are these costumes chosen for June 17? Is there any intrinsic national significance to these outfits that were never even worn on the banks of the Danube?" He then proceeds to pose some pivotal questions:

> *The primary question that arises in my mind is this: Why does the arrangement of this event remain unchanged after 70 years? Has Icelandic culture or intellectual thought not evolved during this time to warrant the introduction of something new? Is this portrayal indicative of the nation's perception of itself in the present moment, or does it merely serve as a collection showcasing how events were organized 70 years ago?*[170]

In many respects, Jökulsson's statements mirror the divisions that have emerged concerning the concept of Iceland as a phenomenon, which is undoubtedly intertwined with the growth of Reykjavík and the process of urbanisation that has unfolded over the past century. It is perhaps a sign of the times that in 2023, after difficult years due to Covid 19, Fish Day in Dalvík was discontinued.

Similar divisions are occurring in various parts of Europe and America, where two contrasting axes of division are at play. On one hand, there are the "liberal" internationalist civic perspectives, which in Iceland are associated with multiculturalism, EU membership, and to some extent, left-wing politics. On the other hand, there are nationalist, conservative viewpoints that oppose European integration but, as mentioned earlier, manifest in diverse ways across the globe.

This division has long been prominently visible in the United States and has been termed the "culture wars" within political and academic discourse. It encompasses viewpoints that can be considered "conservative" or "traditional" as well as those that are deemed "progressive" or "liberal." These perspectives not only have cultural dimensions but also possess geographical affiliations, with liberalism finding a stronghold in the major cities of coastal states such as California, New York, and the New England states, while more conservative values prevail among people in the Central and Southern states. The main issues that divide these groups include abortion, firearms ownership, homosexual rights, religion, immigration, and nationalism. It has been argued that this strain in American politics can be traced back to the British colonial era of the seventeenth and eighteenth centuries, stemming from the development of class divisions within this ostensibly "classless" colony.[171]

This cultural conflict is reflected in Iceland's discourse surrounding regional matters, immigration, gender equality, environmental concerns, whaling, European affairs, transportation, and employment issues, to name a few. Under the leadership of Sigmundur Davíð Gunnlaugsson, the Progressive Party aligned itself closely with conservative stances on these matters, while the Social Democratic Alliance, Björt framtíð, Píratar, and later Viðreisn emerged as the more apparent opposition, espousing contrasting values and positions. This is reflected in the values and concerns of those who identify as voters within these categories, as revealed through polls.

In the realm of politics, the contours of the debate have become particularly distinct in addressing the ideas that have shaped the liberal, multicultural West since the conclusion of World War II and the subsequent resistance to this development.

Examples of such resistance can be seen during Donald Trump's presidency in the United States and in the rhetoric of many populist parties in Europe. This resistance was also evident in the outcome of the referendum on Britain's membership of the European Union in June 2016, where the campaign of those advocating for leaving the union highlighted half-truths and falsehoods.[172] Behind these dynamics lies a longstanding political ideology with roots in the nineteenth century but which gained significant traction in the early twentieth century, with grave consequences: nationalism.

22

Nationalism, the Nordic Countries and Europe

Contrary to the prevailing trend in most other Western countries, nationalism gained ascendancy in Iceland after World War II. This odious ideology, which ultimately led to the Nazi death camps, prompted a complete reconfiguration of European ideology. However, Iceland's experience was different. Instead of grappling with the horrors of war and Nazism, the nation celebrated the establishment of a republic and liberation from Danish rule. Iceland's unique form of nationalism was rooted in a conservative notion of exalting rural society, accompanied by a certain hostility and scepticism toward individual freedom and employment liberties.[173]

Between 1839 and 1850, Icelanders began to view themselves as a distinct nation with inherent rights and corresponding responsibilities. Since then, the pursuit of national freedom has been the overarching objective of Icelandic politics, serving as the guiding principle for the nation's leaders.[174] This period marked the genesis of the independence movement, seeking to sever the ties that had bound Iceland to Denmark for six centuries.

The scholar Sigríður Matthíasdóttir analysed the discourse of prominent figures in Icelandic society during the first half of the twentieth century. She discovered a parallel between Icelandic nationalism and German nineteenth-century nationalism, despite significant differences in external circumstances. In both cases, societies grappled with the demands of their times for economic progress and individualism.[175] Sigríður argues that Icelandic nationalism, much like its German counterpart, aligns with what Hans Kohn and John Plamenatz define as the nationalism of the weak. Although Icelandic society was undoubtedly underdeveloped, the nation possessed a rich literary heritage and a language that had remained relatively unchanged over the centuries. Sigríður contends that these circumstances contributed to aspirations of greatness rooted in a sense of powerlessness.[176]

In a 1996 article on Icelandic nationality, the historian Guðmundur Hálfdanarson asserts that Icelanders have long taken their struggle for independence for granted. They perceive the nation as a natural fact rather than a political idea.[177] According to Hálfdanarson, Icelanders never seriously contemplated that the world could have unfolded in an entirely different manner. Iceland could have become part of a larger Danish state, joined a united Nordic federation, or been assimilated into a major European power. This possibility has remained open for some time (joining the EU), and the reluctance of Icelanders to engage in critical debates about it underscores the strength of Icelandic nationalism, he says.[178]

Hálfdanarson further notes in his 2001 book on the Icelandic nation-state that the resilience of primordial national identity in Iceland is easily explicable. The republic is still young, and the struggle for independence remains vivid in people's minds. Additionally, various conditions in Iceland distinguish it from other European nations.[179]

In his book "Citizens of Europe: The Emergence of a Mass European Identity" (2005), scholar Michel Bruter identifies two types of national identities: civic and cultural. The civic identity stems from the Enlightenment and the French Revolution, linking the legitimacy of political communities to political institutions established through a social contract, as espoused by thinkers from Rousseau to Habermas. On the other hand, the cultural identity, championed by German thinkers like Johann Gottlieb Fichte and Johann Gottfried Herder, connects the legitimacy of political communities to a corresponding "nation" defined by a shared culture and, often, a common language. Given the elusive nature of national discourse in Icelandic politics, the idea of Icelandic identity has been somewhat contorted to relate or integrate with the bourgeois European identity, although Icelanders undoubtedly consider themselves Europeans and cherish their European heritage.[180]

It has been documented that Iceland's stance on European integration bears striking similarities to that of the Nordic countries and the United Kingdom, which occupy special positions in this regard.[181] Peter Lawler draws attention to what he perceives as the internationalist progressivism of the Scandinavian countries (Norway, Denmark, and Sweden), which he believes underpins their claim of being exceptional in the world and opposition to European integration.[182] He argues that the debate on European integration in these countries largely revolves around the future of this "Scandinavian exceptionalism." According to Lawler, the opposition to European integration on these grounds carries a progressive tone but is, in fact, a familiar blend of nostalgic yearning for the past and nationalism.[183]

Iceland's first president, Sveinn Björnsson, addressed a crowd in front of the government residence in Reykjavík after the founding of the Republic in 1944. The photo was found in the author's family album, with the photographer unknown.

Icelandic nationalism exhibits unique characteristics, it lacks the progressiveness often found in other Nordic countries. At times, the idea of Icelandic uniqueness has assumed a peculiar tone, such as when, in 2006, at the hight of the boom before the crash, the Icelandic Chamber of Commerce suggested that

Icelanders should cease comparing themselves to other Nordic countries, as Iceland was superior to them in most aspects.[184]

Nonetheless, the notion of the distinct Icelandic nation, along with the societal structure, poses a significant obstacle to perceiving Iceland as part of the European Union. As Guðmundur Hálfdanarson highlights within a broader European historical context, the Icelandic nation-state developed along relatively traditional lines described by theorists like Ernest Gellner and Miroslav Hroch. Nationalists, led by a small group of intellectuals, transformed a community with a local culture into a nation.[185] This process, which occurred in various forms throughout Europe during the nineteenth and twentieth centuries, resulted in the disintegration of old empires like the Ottoman Empire, Austria-Hungary, and the Russian Empire, shaping the map we have today.

This idea remains prevalent in modern Iceland, where scepticism toward mainstream European politicians and opinion leaders persists regarding the future of the nation-state system and its ability to meet the challenges of the postmodern era.[186] However, there are indications that this sentiment has waned in the second and third decades of the twenty-first century more than ever before in the history of the republic. Multiculturalism has become a more viable entry point for governmental policymaking, as seen in the City of Reykjavík's initiatives, and ideas conflicting with the dominant nationalist policies of the twentieth century have emerged. While some proposals, such as allowing family names, have faced significant resistance and have not been passed by the Althingi (Iceland's parliament), politicians, particularly those on the left, now approach Iceland and its alleged uniqueness with different perspectives than before. Ultimately, nations are social constructs sustained by institutions and discourse as long as they serve a purpose for someone. As Guðmundur Hálfdanarson points out, the way nations are formed is almost coincidental, with circumstances determining one path over another. When nationalism first took hold in Iceland, it clashed with the notion of a Danish nation within the Danish Kingdom to which Iceland belonged, eventually leading to the establishment of Iceland as a distinct nation with its own language—a language that required effort to "revive" and define after centuries of Danish influence.[187]

In many ways, Iceland's Nordic heritage has been its great advantage. The Nordic countries serve as excellent role models for social development, as they consistently rank at the top in terms of quality of life, democracy, human rights, equality, and other factors that contribute to a healthy and happy life. Icelanders have been part of this community for centuries, originating to a significant extent in Scandinavia and speaking a Nordic language. Even after formally severing ties with Denmark, Iceland has diligently cultivated these connections, although the dominance of the Danish language is now being replaced by English as the primary language of communication with the other Nordic countries, at least when there is limited room for misinterpretations.

Icelanders have also received extensive education in the other Nordic countries, and many people have emigrated in search of a better life. Norway has surpassed Denmark as the preferred destination, particularly due to its wealth from oil resources, which provides more material opportunities than elsewhere in the Nordic countries, and its welcoming attitude towards its northern cousins.

The Nordic welfare system has served as a model for Iceland, and many ideas in that respect have been borrowed from other

Nordic countries. This is partly due to similarities in the administrative systems, with Iceland's system having a similar legal basis to Denmark's. However, Icelandic municipalities are not as active as service providers compared to their Nordic counterparts. This can also be attributed to the presence of a third tier of government in the other Nordic countries between the state and municipalities, which is absent in Iceland.

Several cities in the other Nordic countries are comparable in size to Reykjavík. Trondheim has previously been mentioned as sharing similarities with the Reykjavík area. Additionally, cities such as Uppsala and Linköping in Sweden, Aalborg and Odense in Denmark, and Oulu in Finland. Aalborg in northern Jutland is perhaps the closest to Reykjavík when considering population, area, and population density. It also houses several universities, including one similar in size to the University of Iceland, a symphony orchestra, and other amenities typical of well-developed cities of this size.

Cities and towns in the Nordic countries have a special relationship known as twinning associations, which have been in place for decades, fostering various civil society events. Nordic cooperation is not limited to a formal collaboration between governments and administrations; it also includes a robust grassroots partnership involving numerous NGOs, trade unions, political parties, sports clubs, religious movements, and not least individuals.

Formal cooperation should not be underestimated. The Nordic Council holds annual sessions where the main leaders from all Nordic countries meet to decide on important matters. Established in 1952 under the Helsinki Treaty, the Nordic Council operates under the auspices of this treaty, which has been updated several times since. The sessions are held alternately in the five Nordic capitals, taking place in the respective country's parliaments, except for Iceland, where the Althingi is not large enough to host the meeting.

There have long been ideas for closer cooperation among the Nordic countries, including the possibility of becoming one state.[188] Economist Gunnar Wetterberg has explored this subject and highlighted its intriguing aspects. With a population of more than 25 million and a combined GDP that would rank the united Nordic countries among the world's top 10-12 economies, they could exert substantial global influence. As individual small states, they lack access to platforms where major decisions are made, such as the G20. The Nordic values, particularly in environmental matters, are more progressive than those of most large nations, but their impact on the international stage diminishes when divided.

The Nordic countries have taken different paths in the international arena, with EU membership being the most significant point of divergence. Sweden, Denmark, and Finland have joined the European Union, while Norway and Iceland, along with the autonomous territories within the Kingdom of Denmark (Greenland and the Faroe Islands), remain outside. However, Iceland and Norway are members of the European Economic Area (EEA) and the Schengen Area, making them more closely connected to the European Union than any other formally non-member state. It is worth noting that for a long time, Sweden and Finland maintained a "neutral" stance in terms of defence, while Iceland, Denmark, and Norway are NATO members. With the Russian invasion of Ukraine, that has changed, and as of this writing Finland has joined NATO and Sweden is set to join after getting the go-ahead from Turkey, which has been blocking its entrance for domestic political reasons.

23

The European Trajectory

Although Nordic cooperation is important to Iceland, as well as other Nordic countries, the extensive and all-encompassing development of Europe is of utmost importance when it comes to international cooperation. This is not necessarily because European cooperation would be the first emotional option for these countries, as reflected in the "Scandinavian exceptionalism" described above; but because of the enormous underlying economic interests. When Denmark joined what was then called the European Community in 1972, it was described as if the Nordic countries and Nordic cooperation were the youthful love that had the Danish heart, while Europe was the rich wife that all rational reasoning tends to stick to.

The single biggest historical factor that influenced the development of European integration was the Second World War and the tragedy it caused. Nationalism faced an ideological collapse in the extremes of Nazism and the Holocaust. After the war, the voices that wanted to find new ways to the future in Europe grew louder and louder; but the superpowers faced each other across borders that, in many ways, made no sense, so to speak. The basic idea of European integration was to thoroughly integrate Germany into cooperation with other European countries. This would provide the defeated and disgraced power a new entrance into the community of "civilized" countries. Cooperation between France and Germany was not only a focal point but also a matter of interest to the smaller European states. Belgium, the Netherlands, Luxembourg and Italy were full participants along with the countries mentioned above.

Icelanders had long pursued the link with economic integration in Europe. The first institutional channel to it was the membership of the European Free Trade Association (EFTA) in 1970. EFTA was an organisation initially founded by the United Kingdom and a few other smaller countries that wanted the benefits of economic cooperation but did not care for the political overtones of the European Community. However, at this time, Britain had applied for membership of the European Community and would join it, leaving EFTA in 1973.

Later, it can be said that Iceland entered the common market in its entirety with membership of the European Economic Area in 1994, although the country has long resisted the fate of seeking full membership of the European Union. However, that was to change, like so much else, with the Financial Crisis of 2008.

In October 2008, the Icelandic economy was hit hard by the collapse of all of the country's major financial institutions in just a few days. The Icelandic króna also took a heavy blow; it was ripped out of international markets and turned into a currency only usable in Iceland. Although the country's economy has recovered with the unprecedented growth of tourism in recent years, Icelanders are still struggling with the consequences of the economic collapse. The debts of the state and individuals increased, purchasing power collapsed, unemployment reached new heights, and Icelanders' self-confidence took a hit.

The Financial Crisis or "The Collapse" (*Hrunið*) as it is called in Iceland, had various unforeseen consequences. Unrest in politics and protests of an unprecedented magnitude led to the fall of the government of the Independence Party and the Social Democratic Alliance (SDA) in January 2009. The minority government of SDA and the Left Greens took power with the support of the Progressive Party, and parliamentary elections were called in the spring. The results of the parliamentary elections led to the first truly left-wing government of the republican era, which had a parliamentary majority behind it. The results of the ballot box gave SDA, which was the winner of the election, with almost 30% of the vote and 20 (of 63) MPs, an unexpected card up its sleeve in the governmental negotiations with the Left Greens. It also seemed that there was for the first time in history, a parliamentary majority in favour of applying for membership of the European Union. As the Progressive Party had said in the election campaign, it could be understood that it would support a membership application, with conditions, however, and a new political force: the Citizens' Movement founded on the basis of the protest movement in the "Pots-and-Pans" Revolution, (so called because of the pots and pans the protesters banged on outside the Parliament building), had also advocated membership. Progress received 9 MPs in this election, and the Citizens' Movement 4. With 20 MPs from SDA, there were 33 MPs behind the application according to this calculation, in addition to which support could be expected, or at least the abstention, of some MPs from the Independence Party. This meant that the

Left Greens, who had always spoken out against membership, were not in a position to stop this main policy issue of the SDA when writing the government agreement of the second government of Jóhanna Sigurðardóttir in the spring of 2009. Iceland applied for membership of the European Union on 16 July that year. This application was later formally withdrawn by the government, which took over in 2013, so Iceland's reputation as a hesitant and a little bit awkward European was thoroughly reiterated.

However, the most important step in Iceland's European integration was unquestionably taken when Iceland acceded to the Agreement on the European Economic Area (EEA) on 1 January 1994, and thus, de facto, became an associate member of the European Union created by the Maastricht Treaty in 1993. Exactly one year after the entry into force of the EEA agreement, to which Iceland belonged together with the EU countries and the EFTA countries, the fellow EFTAns Sweden, Finland, and Austria became full members of the European Union on 1 January 1995.

Much has been written about the impact of this agreement on the Icelandic economy, but less about the impact on Icelandic self-awareness and culture. A study published by the author of this book in 2014 shows that the word "European" is much more frequently used to refer to Icelanders themselves in the Icelandic media in the first years of this century than what was the case in the twentieth century. Suddenly, opportunities opened up for Icelanders to study and work in other European countries that had previously been limited to the Nordic countries. The Erasmus generation came into being, i.e., the young people who took advantage of new opportunities for exchange studies and began to see themselves in a larger context than before: a European context.

Another major step was taken on the European stage around the turn of the last century. This was when Iceland became part of the Schengen area, which in fact means that the country is within the borders of the European Union in every traditional sense of the word. When someone from America lands in Keflavík, they go through passport control, and after that, they enter the borderless European Union. Iceland is in this respect, more deeply involved in European cooperation than some member states of the European Union. Both the United Kingdom (when it was in the EU) and Ireland, for example, have always been outside of this cooperation.

But what role has Reykjavík played in that story? Formally, it can be said that Reykjavík entered the scene at the turn of the century in 2000 as a full-fledged European city among European cities. That year, Reykjavík was one of the "cultural cities of Europe." The year 2000 was special. It was "The Millennium", the year that everyone wanted to celebrate, and the number of applicants for the honour that year was such that the decision was made to allow nine cities across the continent to carry the title at the turn of the century. Nevertheless, there was great pomp and circumstance in the northernmost capital of the world that year, and cultural events on every corner. On this occasion, the mayor, Ingibjörg Sólrún Gísladóttir said in an article in Morgunblaðið: "Reykjavík has inherited its flourishing culture from the people who grew up in the scattered settlements of the country but had the imagination to dream big dreams, and the endurance to make them come true. The paths of these people lay - and still lie - together in Reykjavík and made the city what it is."

The City of Culture project became extremely extensive.

There were a total of 284 related projects and at least 2,549 events. It is estimated that one and a half million people attended these events during this remarkable year in the city's history. Reykjavík had grown mature and entered the European ballroom.

A lot of water has flowed under the bridge since the turn of the century. Today, Reykjavík is a destination for hundreds of thousands of foreign tourists every year. Accommodation in Reykjavík has multiplied, as previously described. The city of Reykjavík is the gateway into the country, along with being a boiling pot of multiculturalism that has been created in Iceland during the first decades of the new century. This multiculturalism, on the other hand, is a derivative of the steps taken into the European Economic Area in the 1990s and would have been inconceivable without it.

V

The Future

24

Reykjavík and International Politics

In politics, there is a growing trend of cities and municipalities encroaching on areas that were previously under the exclusive jurisdiction of the state. Reykjavík is no exception to this, as demonstrated by the examples provided, and this trend is likely to continue. When US President Donald Trump announced the United States' withdrawal from the Paris Agreement on Combating Climate Change, many mayors in the US reacted by stating that their cities would disregard it and continue working to reduce greenhouse gases as if nothing had changed.[189]

With increased multiculturalism and diversity, the importance of nation-states in shaping people's identities may diminish, particularly in cities where these factors are more pronounced. People may increasingly identify with the cities they live in or grew up in, rather than with the artificial constructs of nations. This connection to the local is explored by author Taiye Selasi in her 2014 TED Talk. She shares her personal experience of being introduced as "from a country" despite feeling a stronger connection to the specific cities in which she has lived and formed relationships. Selasi suggests that evaluating identity based on rituals, relationships, and restrictions can provide a richer and more meaningful understanding of oneself, rather than relying on national clichés and generalisations.[190]

The shift from the national to the local has been widely discussed, with cities gaining increasing relevance in the international arena. Scholar Benjamin Barber, who advocated for greater global unity among cities, notably through initiatives like the Mayor's International Congress, explored this concept until his passing in 2017.[191][192]

Reykjavík, too, has entered this realm, with the city government taking positions on international issues. While examples may exist from earlier times, this development gained momentum during Jón Gnarr's tenure as mayor. Gnarr was unafraid to draw attention to human rights abuses abroad, such as his symbolic act of dressing like the Russian punk band Pussy Riot, as previously mentioned. The City Council also expressed concerns about the treatment of LGBTQ+ individuals in Russia, highlighting the possibility of amending or terminating the cooperation agreement between Reykjavík and Moscow.[193][194]

In December 2023, a group of Palestinian asylum seekers set up camp in front of the Icelandic Parliament, Alþingi, protesting Israel's invasion of the Gaza Strip and demanding asylum for themselves and their families. They did this with the permission of the Reykjavík city government. They were there for a month before the camp was dismantled under pressure from members of the Icelandic government. Photo by the author.

One particular proposal by city representative Björk Vilhelmsdóttir generated significant attention and response. Vilhelmsdóttir put forward a motion to boycott Israeli goods during the Israeli occupation of Palestinian territory. This proposal garnered intense reactions, primarily from the global Jewish community, catching Mayor Dagur B. Eggertsson off guard. The mayor expressed surprise that this issue received more international attention than Iceland's recognition of the Palestinian state in 2011. Following the strong backlash, the mayor announced that the proposal would be withdrawn at the next city council meeting, where unanimous proposals were presented to officially retract the boycott agreement.[195][196]

In some ways, this incident reflects Reykjavík's growing influence and brand strength. While it may be premature to label the city as cosmopolitan, it is undoubtedly becoming increasingly relevant. Interestingly, its actions in this case garnered more attention than those of the small state of Iceland. The fallout from this case may impact Reykjavík's future willingness to engage in international affairs.

25

The Lessons from Living in Harsh and Remote Areas

Most of the people interviewed for this book express optimism about the Reykjavík metropolitan area. They believe that it is successful and well-positioned to compete internationally for both people and companies. However, there are several obstacles to overcome. These include the need for university education in English, a more agile administration for services to new residents, and improved public transportation. The city authorities and others involved in these aspects have a positive attitude towards immigrants. Other challenges, such as weather and the distance from other metropolitan areas, are more difficult to address. However, transportation to and from the city has improved with the increase in tourism. Regarding the weather, it may require a change in mindset. The name of the country itself does not help in that respect either.

Sometimes it is possible to go ice-skating on the pond. Photo by the author.

As discussed in the chapter on climate, the weather in Reykjavík is not worse than in many other places where people reside. For example, in Helsinki, temperatures can drop below -30 degrees Celsius during the coldest months. Nonetheless, Iceland has a volatile climate that affects human life and organisation. The city's future, as well as its overall quality of life, depends on finding innovative ways to mitigate the impact of the weather on its residents. This must go hand in hand with reducing the reliance on private cars, which are costly and dangerous, and encouraging the use of public transportation and other environmentally friendly means of travel. However, to make public transport more attractive, it needs to be convenient, frequent, and competitive with the comfort offered by cars, such as shelter from the elements. This is a key challenge for local authorities in the capital area and an essential step towards increased sustainability.

In many aspects, Iceland is an interesting example of creating a competitive and prosperous society in challenging conditions, where neighbouring countries are far away. Despite this, Iceland has established a welfare state with a high degree of equality, prosperity, and democratic governance. Children are well taken care of, and there are ample opportunities for education, development, and leisure activities, including sports and culture, comparable to the best in the world. This achievement is not solely attributable to the Icelandic nation itself, but rather to the human spirit. Icelanders are not fundamentally different from people in other parts of the world. While they can be defined as a group based on language, passports, and place of residence, they are fundamentally the same as other individuals. However, Iceland's success is also rooted in the wise utilisation of its valuable resources and the country's stable and democratic community. Icelanders have been peaceful and friendly, engaging in profitable trade with neighbouring countries, which directly contributes to their prosperity. It is hoped that this positive dynamic will continue, as Iceland's well-being depends on the success and peaceful coexistence with its neighbours.

What lessons can be learned from the story of Reykjavík? Firstly, communities can thrive almost anywhere if properly nurtured. Secondly, creating vibrant and dynamic cities does not necessarily require large populations. However, the key to success lies in good communication and connection with other communities. Despite the distances, Iceland maintains frequent and regular transportation connections with the rest of the world. The influx of visitors enriches human life and the economy, while Icelanders themselves bring back ideas and trends from abroad. As a European country, Iceland and its capital, Reykjavík, are part of a much larger cultural world beyond the confines of the island. Without this connectivity, their existence would be fundamentally different.

Simultaneously, a viable modern life in Iceland would be inconceivable without Reykjavík. The city is where the majority of Icelanders reside, where Icelandic culture flourishes, and where the fate of the nation is determined. It serves as a bulwark against the emigration of young people, which is evident in the smaller communities of the Faroe Islands, and Greenland. These places lack comparable cities to satisfy the aspirations of young people for an exciting and diverse life. As discussed in this book, the role of the city in this context is not without controversy. The tension between the capital and the idea of a more conservative society based on nationality and primary production, as well as equal residence throughout the country, represents an Icelandic version of the cultural divide seen in the Western world. Reykjavík, located in the southwest corner, represents the vibrant city against alternative visions. Iceland needs both elements to thrive: a strong and exciting city as a bulwark against depopulation and as a cultural melting pot, while also preserving settlements throughout the country to harness the gifts of nature and maintain a connection with Icelandic roots. Without this balance, the city would struggle to thrive.

This book has covered a wide range of topics, although not always in great depth. The focus has been on shedding light on the mosaic of Reykjavík, how it reflects contemporary society, its connections to other human settlements, its natural and climatic context, and the characteristics of its inhabitants in the "northernmost capital in the world." The city has experienced rapid growth and is once again at a crossroads. Its opportunities lie in taking even more significant strides towards the development of the Reykjavík area as a whole. Efforts thus far have focused on planning, marketing, and certain service aspects, but more substantial steps should be taken in administration. This includes strengthening existing units that serve the citizens and addressing the democratic deficit that arises when services are outsourced to companies owned by multiple municipalities, as is currently the case in waste management and public transportation.

Some may argue that having one municipality containing two-thirds of the country's population, while all other municipalities are comparatively small, is undesirable. However, this argument does not hold up when considering the advantages of having the capital area as a single municipality. Reykjavík is already significantly larger than other municipalities in the country, and merging them would not result in a substantial change in that regard. It is in the best interest of all Icelanders to operate the city in the most efficient and effective way possible. Maintaining six or seven municipalities within the same city and having multiple institutions when a stronger and more unified approach is feasible is unnecessary.

Overall, Icelanders are fortunate to have built a city that lives up to its name, despite historical resistance from the ruling class. Fortunately, this resistance has not stifled the city's growth or prevented it from becoming a remarkable place at the edge of the inhabited world. Reykjavík, the northernmost capital in the world and the fourteenth largest urban area in the Nordic countries is full of energy, uniqueness, and innovative ideas. May it continue to prosper and thrive for centuries to come.

Epilogue

It was around the age of eighteen that I suddenly began to take notice of the city I had grown up in: Reykjavík. Previously, it had simply served as a backdrop to my life, without its own distinct existence. But at this age, it was as if a veil had been lifted from my eyes, and I started to see the vibrant colours of the city more clearly. I began to appreciate the beauty in the concrete structures, the streets, the small patches of greenery squeezed between sidewalks. Perhaps the city's 200th anniversary in 1986 played a role in this awakening - all the discussions, pop songs, celebrations made us residents feel like the city was truly coming into its own, becoming a "real city." It could also be attributed to growing older, gaining maturity; the child within me receding, and an adult with an eye for beauty emerging.

The author on "Rainbow Street" in Reykjavík or Skólavörðustígur as it is formally named. Photo by Sema Severin.

I also recall a few years later, after returning from a month-long journey across mainland Europe, the so-called Interrail trip. I had traveled through Germany, France, Italy, Switzerland, and Austria, and when I came back to Reykjavík, I felt a distinct difference between the cities I had visited and the one on the island in the North Atlantic where I resided. Most of the cities I had seen had a certain common character, a distinctiveness that set them apart from Reykjavík. The houses in Reykjavík were smaller, with less emphasis on pedestrian areas and less developed public transportation. But despite that, the same feeling that had sparked in 1986 persisted. The colours seemed brighter, the presence of summer more vivid, and the architecture more chaotic.

This led me to reflect on how Reykjavík was during my youth, particularly the seventies. In recollection, Reykjavík was dirtier, uglier, and colder back then. The streets were paved with slabs and gravel, and litter was commonly thrown out of car windows. Broken glass, chewing gum, and cigarette butts could be found everywhere. Downtown was mostly empty, except for the unfortunate and teenagers. The vegetation seemed sparse, and the wind mercilessly whipped through the streets, making a small figure in a hooded coat feel the onslaught of horizontal rain from all sides. Of course, this portrayal is somewhat exaggerated and subjective. There were still good days in the seventies, although not many.

This book is about my city, Reykjavík. It probably hasn't escaped the reader's attention that, in my mind, Reykjavík encompasses the entire metropolitan area, including all the municipalities in the capital region. After all, I grew up in Kópavogur and lived in Hafnarfjörður for over a decade before moving to Vesturbær, where I had also resided during my undergraduate studies. When foreigners ask me if I live in Reykjavík, I always answer without hesitation, "Yes." However, in other more domestic situations, I identify myself as being from Kópavogur of course.

Notes

PREFACE

1. https://www.skra.is/um-okkur/frettir/frett/2023/08/22/Hlutfall-erlendra-rikisborgara-eftir-sveitarfelogum-og-landshlutum-i-agust-2023/
2. Sigrún Birgisdóttir og Massimo Santanicchia, *Reykjavíkurgötur 2010: Sóleyjargata, Fríkirkjuvegur, Lækjargata* (Reykjavík: Listaháskóli Íslands, 2010).
3. UNESCO, "Reykjavik, Iceland: UNESCO City of Literature", Creative Cities Network, 2011, http://www.unesco.org/new/en/culture/themes/creativity/creative-cities-network/literature/reykjavik/.
4. "10 Cities That Are Shaping The Future Of Urban Living", The Huffington Post, 5 2015, http://www.huffingtonpost.com/2015/05/11/future-cities-urban-planning_n_7222018.html.
5. "Hjólaborgin Reykjavík" (Reykjavík: Reykjavíkurborg, febrúar 2010), http://reykjavik.is/sites/default/files/skjol_thjonustulysingar/hjolreidaa___tlun_LOW_OK.pdf. p. 14.
6. Peter Hall, "Shangri-La of the North?", *Town & Country Planning*, júní 2001.
7. "Heildarfjöldi erlendra ferðamanna ", *Ferðamálastofa*, 2020, https://www.ferdamalastofa.is/is/tolur-og-utgafur/fjoldi-ferdamanna/heildarfjoldi-erlendra-ferdamanna.
8. "Íslensk ferðaþjónusta" (Reykjavík: Íslandsbanki, mars 2015), https://www.islandsbanki.is/library/Skrar/Fyrirtaeki/Ferdatjonustuskyrsla.PDF.

THE TRIUMPH OF THE CITIES

9. Hariri, Yuval Noah. "Sapiens: A Brief History of Humankind." Vintage, 2014.
10. Hardt, Michael, and Antonio Negri. "Empire." Harvard University Press, 2001.
11. Davidson, Helen. "London's Post-Brexit Bid to Become an Independent City State." The Guardian, 7 July 2016.

12 Dunford, Michael, and David S. A. Gabbard. "Cities and Globalization." Routledge, 2012.

13 Barber, Benjamin R. "If Mayors Ruled the World: Dysfunctional Nations, Rising Cities." Yale University Press, 2013.

14 World Congress of Mayors. "The Hague World Congress of Mayors." Accessed June 2023.

15 Ibid.

16 Ibid.

17 Jacobs, Jane. "The Economy of Cities." Vintage Books, 1970.

WHAT IS A CITY?

18 "Kópavogur verður ekki að borg - tillagan féll á jöfnu", *visir.is*, 14. september 2011, visir.is útgáfa, http://www.visir.is/kopavogur-verdur-ekki-ad-borg—-tillagan-fell-a-jofnu/article/2011110919539

19 "Verður Akureyri næsta borg á Íslandi? Tímaspursmál, segir borgarstjóri", *eyjan.pressan.is*, 30. ágúst 2012, Eyjan-Pressan útgáfa, http://eyjan.pressan.is/frettir/2012/08/30/verdur-akureyri-naesta-borg-a-islandi-timaspursmal-segir-borgarstjori/.

20 Barber, *If Mayors Ruled the World; Dysfunctional Nations, Rising Cities.*

21 Ibid.

22 During the Covid pandemic of 2020-2022, there was a period that suggested that this tide had turned, but of course it hadn't.

23 Michael P. Todaro og Stephen C. Smith, *Economic Development, Eleventh Edition* (Harlow: Pearson Education Limited, 2011), pp. 311-355.

24 Ibid. p. 322.

25 Sigurður Snævarr, *Haglýsing Íslands* (Reykjavík: Heimskringla, 1993).

26 "State of the Nordic Region 2013", Nordregio Report (Stockholm: Nordregio, 2014).

27 "Population density (people per sq. km of land area)", World Bank, 2017, http://data.worldbank.org/indicator/EN.POP.DNST?year_high_desc=false.

28 https://www.samband.is/sveitarfelogin/#tab2

DOES SIZE MATTER?

29 "Largest Metropolitan Areas in the Nordic Countries", *Wikipedia, the Free Encyclopedia*, 10. október 2014, http://en.wikipedia.org/w/index.php?title=

Largest_metropolitan_areas_in_the_Nordic_countries&oldid=628088 538.

30 "2011 Census: Population and household estimates for the United Kingdom" (Office for National Statistics, 17. December 2012).

31 "List of Metropolitan Areas in Europe", *Wikipedia, the Free Encyclopedia*, 18. október 2014, http://en.wikipedia.org/w/index.php?title=List_of_met ropolitan_areas_in_Europe&oldid=624891285.

32 Gunnar Helgi Kristinsson, *Íslenska stjórnkerfið*, 2nd ed. (Reykjavík: Háskóli Íslands, 2007).

33 Snævarr, *Haglýsing Íslands*.

34 Ibid.

35 The Economist, "Reykjavik-on-Thames", *The Economist*, January 2009, http://www.economist.com/node/13021969.

36 Gunnar Karlsson, "Af hverju voru yfirvöld á Íslandi áður á móti borgarsamfélagi og Reykjavík?", Vísindavefurinn, 29. júní 2001, http://www.visindav efur.is/svar.php?id=1754.

37 "Spá um mannfjölda 2013–2060", Hagtíðindi; Statistical Series (Hagstofan, 22. ágúst 2013), https://hagstofa.is/lisalib/getfile.aspx?ItemID=15409 .

38 "Aðalskipulag Reykjavíkur 2010 - 2030" (Reykjavíkurborg, Jún 2014), http://issuu.com/skipulag/docs/20130802_ar_a5_isl_vef.

39 Richard Florida, "What Cities Really Need to Attract Entrepreneurs, According to Entrepreneurs", 2 November 2014, http://www.citylab.com/wo rk/2014/02/what-cities-really-need-attract-entrepreneurs-according-e ntrepreneurs/8349/.

40 Mario Polèse, *The Wealth and Poverty of Regions: Why Cities Matter* (Chicago: University of Chicago, 2009).

41 Gallup.com, "Potential Net Migration Index Declines in Many Countries", Gallup.com, 17 January 2014, http://www.gallup.com/poll/166796/potenti al-net-migration-index-declines-countries.aspx.

REYKJAVÍK IN COMPARISON WITH SIMILAR CITIES

42 Mail Online, "Iceland: Smaller population than Bournemouth... but they beat Holland!", Mail Online, 14 October 2014, http://www.dailymail.co.uk/ sport/football/article-2792328/iceland-smaller-population-bournemout h-beat-holland-taking-euro-2016-qualifying-storm.html.

43 "Own goals", *The Economist*, viewed 10 May 2016, http://www.economist.com/news/britain/21707899-englands-football-manager-sent-cyclists-face-questions-about-drug-use-own-goals.

44 "Urban Population", world.bymap.org, 2015, http://world.bymap.org/UrbanPopulation.html.

45 "Bournemouth", *Wikipedia, the Free Encyclopedia*, 10 December 2014, http://en.wikipedia.org/w/index.php?title=Bournemouth&oldid=637008961.

46 Ibid.

47 "Trondheim", *Wikipedia, the Free Encyclopedia*, 11 December 2014, http://en.wikipedia.org/w/index.php?title=Trondheim&oldid=635117052.

48 "Agglomeration Community of the Grenoble Alpes Métropole", *Wikipedia, the Free Encyclopedia*, 11 December 2014, http://en.wikipedia.org/w/index.php?title=Agglomeration_community_of_the_Grenoble_Alpes_M%C3%A9tropole&oldid=544629809.

49 "Grenoble", *Wikipedia, the Free Encyclopedia*, 11 December 2014, http://en.wikipedia.org/w/index.php?title=Grenoble&oldid=635776878.

50 "List of French Regions and Overseas Collectivities by GDP", *Wikipedia, the Free Encyclopedia*, 10 December 2014, http://en.wikipedia.org/w/index.php?title=List_of_French_regions_and_overseas_collectivities_by_GDP&oldid=631618132.

51 Polèse, *The Wealth and Poverty of Regions: Why Cities Matter*.

52 Ibid.

53 Edward Glaeser, *Triumph of the City; How Urban Spaces make us Human* (London: Macmillan, 2011).

54 Ibid.

55 "Nemendur", https://www.hi.is/kynningarefni/nemendur.

56 "Blue Banana", ed, https://en.wikipedia.org/wiki/Blue_Banana.

57 "Cycling in The Hague", Vefsíða borgaryfirvalda, The Hague, 12 March 2010, http://www.denhaag.nl/en/residents/getting-there-and-around/to/Cycling-in-The-Hague-1.htm.

58 Consideration is underpinned by the fact that cyclists and pedestrians always have the right of way if there is an accident involving them and the cars.

NATURE AND CLIMATE

59 https://www.vedur.is/vedur/frodleikur/greinar/nr/1060
60 vedur.is, "Mánaðarmeðaltöl fyrir stöð 1 - Reykjavík", vedur.is, viewed 15 December 2014, http://www.vedur.is/Medaltalstoflur-txt/Stod_001_Rey kjavik.ManMedal.txt.
61 Glaeser, *Triumph of the City; How Urban Spaces make us Human*.
62 Magnús Jónsson og Sigurður Harðarson, *Veðurfar og byggt umhverfi*, Ritröð um vistvænar áherslur í byggðu umhverfi (Reykjavík: Arkitektafélag Íslands, Vistmennt, 2014).
63 "The Hague", Wikipedia page, 2017, https://en.wikipedia.org/wiki/The_H ague.
64 Skógræktarfélag Íslands, "Græni trefillinn, skýrsla til stjórnar Sambands sveitarfélaga á höfuðborgarsvæðinu (SSH)" (Reykjavík, October 2006), http://skog.is/images/stories/verkefni/gtskyrsla2006.pdf.
65 Magnús Jónsson og Sigurður Harðarson, *Veðurfar og byggt umhverfi*.
66 Ibid.
67 Ibid.
68 Ibid.
69 Orkuveita Reykjavíkur, "Saga heita vatnsins", or.is, ed, http://www.or.is/s ites/default/files/saga_heita_vatnsins.pdf.
70 Rögnvaldur Guðmundsson, "Erlendir ferðamenn í Reykjavík 2004-2013 – samanburður og þróun. Samantekt unnin fyrir Höfuðborgarstofu, desember 2013" (Reykjavík: Rannsóknir og ráðgjöf ferðaþjónustunnar, December 2013), http://visitreykjavik.is/sites/default/files/erlendir_ferda menn_i_reykjavik_2004-2013_samanburdur_og_throun.pdf. p. 4.

A DANISH OUTPOST

71 Snorri Baldursson, *Lífríki Íslands, vistkerfi lands og sjávar* (Reykjavík: Opna og Forlagið, 2014), p. 70.
72 "Miðaldadómkirkja í Skálholti - Stórvirki í íslenskri menningarsögu endurreist -" (kirkjan.is, October 2011), http://kirkjan.is/kerfi/skraars ofn/kirkjan-frettir/2011/11/greinargerd-okt-2011.pdf.
73 Trausti Valsson, *Reykjavík vaxtarbroddur; Þróun höfuðborgar* (Reykjavík: Fjölva útgáfa, 1986).
74 Ibid.
75 "Kaupstaður", Wikipedia, frjálsa alfræðiritið, 2015, https://is.wikipedia.or g/wiki/Kaupsta%C3%B0ur.

76 EA Gutkind, *Urban Development in the Alpine and Scandinavian Countries*, b. Vol. II, International History of City Development (New York: The Free Press, 1965).

77 Ibid.

78 Birgit Sawyer og Peter Sawyer, *Medieval Scandinavia*, b. Vol. 17, The Nordic Series (Minneapolis: University of Minnesota Press, 1993).

79 https://en.wikipedia.org/wiki/Kattegat

80 Gutkind, *Urban Development in the Alpine and Scandinavian Countries*.

81 Else Roesdahl, *Bolig og Familie i Danmarks Middlelalder* (Hoejbjerg: Jysk Arkeologisk Selskab, 2003).

82 Gutkind, *Urban Development in the Alpine and Scandinavian Countries*.

83 Ibid.

84 Ibid.

85 Ibid.

86 Sawyer og Sawyer, *Medieval Scandinavia*.

87 Ibid.

88 Ibid.

89 Ibid.

90 Baldur Thorhallsson og Þorsteinn Kristjánsson, "Iceland's External Affairs from 1400 to the Reformation: Anglo-German Economic and Societal Shelter in a Danish Political Vacuum", *Stjórnmál og stjórnsýsla* 9, tbl. 1 (2013): 113–37.

91 "Hyllingarbréf Íslendinga til Eiríks konungs af Pommern", júl 1419, Íslenzkt fornbréfasafn IV (Kaupmannahöfn 1897).

92 Thorhallsson og Kristjánsson, "Iceland's External Affairs from 1400 to the Reformation: Anglo-German Economic and Societal Shelter in a Danish Political Vacuum".

THE BIRTH OF A CAPITAL

93 "Hafnarfjörður", *Wikipedia, frjálsa alfræðiritið*, 28. janúar 2015, http://is.wikipedia.org/w/index.php?title=Hafnarfj%C3%B6r%C3%B0ur&oldid=1478523.

94 "Bessastaðir", 2015, http://www.forseti.is/Bessastadir/.

95 "Viðey: Saga", *Viðey* (blog), 2015, http://videy.com/videy/saga/.

CONCRETE AND PARKING SPOTS

96 Eiríkur Rögnvaldsson, "Landnámabók (Sturlubók)", Netútgáfan, 1998, http://www.snerpa.is/net/snorri/landnama.htm.

97 "Gatan sem borgarrými", reykavik.is, 2010, http://eldri.reykjavik.is/deskt opdefault.aspx/tabid-2374/6213_view-2235/.

98 Ibid.

99 "Höfuðborgarsvæðið 2040, tillaga til auglýsingar 22. ágúst 2014", Issuu, 2014, http://issuu.com/ssh.is/docs/throunaraaetlun_2015-2018_17_04_201.

100 "Svæðisskipulag höfuðborgarsvæðisins 2001-2024" (Reykjavík: Samvinnunefnd um svæðisskipulag á höfuðborgarsvæðinu, 2001), http://reykjavi k.is/sites/default/files/skjol_thjonustulysingar/fylgiriti_byggdin_landsl agid.pdf.

101 Sigrún Birgisdóttir og Santanicchia, *Reykjavíkurgötur 2010: Sóleyjargata, Fríkirkjuvegur, Lækjargata*.

102 Visir.is, "Isavia falið að loka flugbraut 06/24", 30. júní 2016, http://www.v isir.is/isavia-falid-ad-loka-flugbraut-06-24/article/2016160639847.

103 "Flugvallarkostir á höfuðborgarsvæðinu, sameiginleg athugun ríkis, Reykjavíkurborgar og Icelandair Group" (Reykjavík: Skýrsla stýrihóps, Jún 2015), http://www.visir.is/assets/pdf/XZ1885625.PDF.

THE TOWN BY THE BLUE CHANNELS

104 Gunnar Thoroddsen, "Knud Zimsen fyrrverandi borgarstjóri, minningarorð", 21. apríl 1953, Morgunblaðið útgáfa.

105 "Of seint", *Morgunblaðið*, ma 1920.

106 Ibid.

107 "Meðmæli með Zimsen", *Alþýðublaðið*, ma 1920.

108 "Aldarafmæli embættis borgarstjóra", *Morgunblaðið*, 5. júní 2008, mbl. is útgáfa, http://www.mbl.is/frettir/innlent/2008/05/06/aldarafmaeli_emb aettis_borgarstjora/.

109 "Þingmannaförin 1906 og konungskoman 1907", Heimastjórn í 100 ár, 2004, http://www.heimastjorn.is/heimastjornartiminn/thingmannaforin-og-konungskoman/.

110 Civis, "Páll Einarsson, borgarstjóri í Reykjavík", *Sunnanfari*, Ma 1913.

111 "Hundrað ár frá kjöri fyrsta borgarstjórans", *Morgunblaðið*, 5. júlí 2008, http://www.mbl.is/greinasafn/grein/1212530/.

NOTES

THE LONG REIGN OF THE INDEPENDENCE PARTY
112 https://www.althingi.is/altext/cv/is/?nfaerslunr=25

THE CITY FLOURISHES
113 "Meirihlutinn andvígur ráðhúsi við Tjörnina", *DV*, 17 November 1987.

114 "Kosningasaga, upplýsingasíða um kosningar á Íslandi", Reykjavík 1986, viewed 23 November 2016, https://kosningasaga.wordpress.com/sveitarstjornarkosningar/hofudborgarsvaedid/reykjavik/reykjavik-til-1994/reykjavik-1986/.

THE REYKJAVÍK LIST
115 "Sameiginlegur listi mundi kolfella sjálfstæðismenn", *DV*, 17 January 1994.

THE BEST PARTY
116 "Jón Gnarr stofnar stjórnmálaflokk", *visir.is*, 16 November 2009, http://www.visir.is/jon-gnarr-stofnar-stjornmalaflokk/article/2009485732613.

117 Ibid.

118 Ibid.

119 Tyrfingur Tyrfingsson, "Jón Gnarr og listaverk hans, Besti flokkurinn" (Listaháskóli Íslands, 2011), http://skemman.is/stream/get/1946/8561/23303/1/Lokaritgerd.pdf. p. 5.

THE REYKJAVÍKIANS AND THEIR NEIGHBOURS
120 Óskar Dýrmundur Ólafsson, interview,, 21 February 2017.

121 Ibid.

122 "Fólkið í skugganum, athugun á högum lakast settu borgarbúanna" (Reykjavík: Rauði krossinn í Reykjavík, 2016), https://www.raudikrossinn.is/media/deildir/folkidiskugganumnetone.pdf., p. 13.

123 Ibid.

124 Erla Björk Sigurðardóttir, "Kortlagning á fjölda og högum útigangsfólks í Reykjavík" (Reykjavík: Velferðarsvið Reykjavíkurborgar, september 2012), http://reykjavik.is/sites/default/files/ymis_skjol/skjol_utgefid_efni/kortlagning_fjoelda_og_hoegum_utangar_sf_lks.pdf.

IMMIGRATION
125 Jennifer Brown, "Expressions of Diasporic Belonging: The Divergent Emotional Geographies of Britain's Polish Communities", *Emotion, Space*

and Society 4, tbl. 4 (2011): 229–37, https://doi.org/10.1016/j.emospa.2011. 01.004.

126 Álfrún Sigurgeirsdóttir og Unnur Dís Skaptadóttir, "Polish construction workers in Iceland; Rights and perceptions of inequalities at building sites", Félags- og mannvísindadeild, ritstjórar: Ása Guðný Ásgeirsdóttir, Helga Björnsdóttir og Helga Ólafs, Október 2011, pp. 8–14.

127 https://px.hagstofa.is/pxis/pxweb/is/Ibuar/Ibuar__mannfjoldi__3_bak grunnur__Faedingarland/MAN12103.px/table/tableViewLayout2/

128 Eva Heiða Önnudóttir og Njörður Sigurjónsson, "Kynþáttahyggja og viðhorf til innflytjenda á Íslandi; Könnun meðal íslenskra ríkisborgara á kynþáttahyggju og viðhorfum þeirra til innflytjenda á Íslandi" (Borgarnes: Rannsóknamiðstöð Háskólans á Bifröst, October 2008).

129 "Lykiltölur mannfjöldans 1703-2014", Vefsíða Hagstofu Íslands, hagstofan.is, 2014, hagstofan.is.

130 Vísindavefurinn, "Hversu margir væru Íslendingar ef allar þessar hamfarir hefðu ekki gengið yfir okkur frá landnámi?", Vísindavefurinn, 9 February 2014, http://www.visindavefur.is/svar.php?id=67695.

131 "Emigrationen från Sverige till Nordamerika", *Wikipedia*, 2015, http://sv. wikipedia.orghttp://sv.wikipedia.org/w/index.php?title=Emigrationen_fr %C3%A5n_Sverige_till_Nordamerika&oldid=28723914.

132 Zygmunt Bauman, *Wasted Lives; Modernity and its Outcasts* (Cambridge: Polity, 2004), p. 4.

133 Ibid. p. 6.

134 https://assets.ctfassets.net/8k0h54kbe6bj/6iBz1zUuaMsuvYj0iM2Mh3/33 22d942cf44d83c805fa46521146865/T__lfr____i_verndarsvi__s_202 2.pdf

135 Frédéric Docquier, Çağlar Ozden, og Giovanni Peri, "The Labour Market Effects of Immigration and Emigration in OECD Countries", *The Economic Journal* 124, tbl. 579 (1 September 2014): 1106–45, https://doi.org/10.1111/e coj.12077.

136 Ibid.

DOUBLE RESIDENCY

137 Anthony M. Orum og Xiangmin Chen, *The World of Cities; Places in Comparative and Historical Perspective*, 21st Century Sociology (Malden: Blackwell Publishing, 2003).

138 Bernd Upmeyer, *Binational Urbanism; On the Road to Paradise* (trancity*valiz, 2015).

139 "Innflytjendur í Reykjavík eftir hverfum 1998-2019", hagstofa.is, 2020, http://px.hagstofa.is/pxis/pxweb/is/Ibuar/Ibuar__mannfjoldi__3_bakgrunnur__Uppruni/MAN43006.px/.

140 Bernd Upmeyer, *Binational Urbanism; On the Road to Paradise* (trancity*valiz, 2015).

141 Florida, Richard, (2002), The Rise of the Creative Class, (Basic Books; New York)

142 https://news.gallup.com/migration/interactive.aspx

A PROMISED LAND

143 "Canada's immigration policy No country for old men", *The Economist*, 1. október 2015, http://www.economist.com/news/americas/21638191-canada-used-prize-immigrants-who-would-make-good-citizens-now-people-job-offers-have.

144 "Canada's Settlement and Integration Model" (Immigration, Refugees and Citizenship Canada, mars 2017), p. 2.

145 "Integration of Immigrants; Issue: An overview of immigrant integration in Canada" (Canadian Embassy in Reykjavík, Apríll 2017).

146 Ibid.

147 Ibid.

148 Anne-Tamara Lorre, Interview, 4 March 2017.

149 Ibid.

150 "Facts and figures 2014 – Immigration overview: Permanent residents" (Government of Canada, 2014), http://www.cic.gc.ca/english/resources/statistics/facts2014/permanent/01.asp.

151 "NHS Profile, Toronto, C, Ontario 2011" (Statistics Canada, 2011), https://www12.statcan.gc.ca/nhs-enm/2011/dp-pd/prof/details/page.cfm?Lang=E&Geo1=CSD&Code1=3520005&Data=Count&SearchText=toronto&SearchType=Begins&SearchPR=01&A1=All&B1=All&Custom=&TABID=1.

152 "Immigration to Israel: Total Immigration, by Country per Year (1948 - Present)" (Jewish Virtual Library, 2013), https://www.jewishvirtuallibrary.org/jsource/Immigration/immigration_by_country2.html.

DESTINATION REYKJAVÍK

153 Hallfríður Þórarinsdóttir, Sólveig H. Georgsdóttir, og Berglind L. Hafsteinsdóttir, "Staða innflytjenda á erfiðleikatímum - raddir og viðhorf" (Reykjavík: MIRRA, miðstöð um innflytjendarannsóknir, ReykjavíkurAkademíunni, Rauða krossinum, 2009), http://mirra.is/Stada_innflytjenda_heild.pdf, p. 73.

154 "Fólkið í skugganum, athugun á högum lakast settu borgarbúanna" (Reykjavík: Rauði krossinn í Reykjavík, 2016), https://www.raudikrossinn.is/media/deildir/folkidiskugganumnetone.pdf., p. 14.

155 Ibid.

156 https://www.asi.is/media/318371/islenskur-vinnumarkadur-2023.pdf

157 https://icc.bak-economics.com/

158 Intercultural Cities, "Reykjavik: Results of the Intercultural Cities Index. A comparison between 64 cities1" (Intercultural Cities, september 2014), https://rm.coe.int/CoERMPublicCommonSearchServices/DisplayDCTMContent?documentId=09000016802ff6de.

159 Anna Kristinsdóttir, Interview, 17 January 2017.

160 Ibid.

161 Ibid.

A CLASH OF CULTURES

162 "Reykjavik Pride", REYKJAVIK PRIDE, 2014, http://www.reykjavikpride.com/.

163 "Fiskidagurinn", Fiskidagurinn mikli, 2014, http://www.fiskidagurinnmikli.is/is/fiskidagurinn.

164 "Styttist í Fiskidaginn mikla", 8 2012, mbl. is útgáfa, http://www.mbl.is/frettir/innlent/2012/08/07/styttist_i_fiskidaginn_mikla/.

165 Christine Ingebritsen, *The Nordic States and European Unity* (Ithaca: Cornell University Press, 1998), pp. 172-3.

166 "Cities and Brexit", CityCommentary (blog), 27 June 2016, http://cityobservatory.org/cities-and-brexit/.

167 Barber, *If Mayors Ruled the World; Dysfunctional Nations, Rising Cities*.

168 DV, "Forsætisráðuneytið borgar fjórum sinnum meira fyrir skagfirskan kór", DV, ma 2014, http://www.dv.is/frettir/2014/5/9/forsaetisraduneytid-borgar-fyrir-skagfirskan-kor-G63H8Q/.

169 Illugi Jökulsson, "Facebook síða Illuga Jökulssonar", júní 2014, https://www.facebook.com/illugi.

170 Ibid.

171 Nancy Isenberg, *White Trash: The 400-Year Untold History of Class in America* (New York: Penguin Books, 2017).

172 "EU referendum: Immigration and Brexit - what lies have been spread?", *The Independent*, 6 2016, http://www.independent.co.uk/news/uk/politics/eu-referendum-immigration-and-brexit-what-lies-have-been-spread-a7092521.html.

NATIONALISM, THE NORDIC COUNTRIES AND EUROPE

173 Eiríkur Bergmann, *Sjálfstæð þjóð; Trylltur skríll og landráðalýður* (Reykjavík: Veröld, 2011).

174 Guðmundur Hálfdanarson, *Íslenska þjóðríkið - uppruni og endimörk* (Reykjavík: Hið íslenska bókmenntafélag, 1996), p. 27.

175 Sigríður Matthíasdóttir, "Réttlæting þjóðernis. Samanburður á alþýðufyrirlestrum Jóns Aðils og hugmyndum Johanns Gottlieb Fichte", *Skírnir* Vor (1995): 36–64., p. 51.

176 Ibid.

177 Guðmundur Hálfdanarson, "Hvað gerir Íslendinga að þjóð? Nokkrar hugleiðingar um uppruna og eðli þjóðernis.", *Skírnir*, 1996, p. 27.

178 Ibid.

179 Guðmundur Hálfdanarson, *Íslenska þjóðríkið - uppruni og endimörk*, p. 9

180 Guðmundur Hálfdanarson, "Iceland and Europe", í *European Peripheries in Interaction. The Nordic Countries and the Iberian Peninsula*, Ritstjórar: L. Beltrán, J. Maestro, & L. Salo-Lee (Alcalá: Universidad de Alcalá, 2002), 333–47.

181 Magnús Árni Magnússon, "Nordic and British Reluctance towards European Integration, MPhil Thesis" (University of Cambridge, 2000).

182 Peter Lawler, "Scandinavian Exceptionalism and European Union", *Journal of Common Market Studies* 35 (1997): 565–94, p. 566.

183 Ibid.

184 "Viðskiptaþing Ísland 2015" (Viðskiptaráð, 2006), http://vi.is/%C3%BAtg%C3%A1fa/sk%C3%BDrslur/2006_02_08%20Island_2015.pdf., p. 22

185 Guðmundur Hálfdanarson, "Iceland and Europe".

186 Ibid.

187 Guðmundur Hálfdanarson, "Language, Identity and Political Integration. Iceland in the Age of Enlightenment", í *Vid gränsen. Integration och*

identiteter i det förnationella Norden, Makadam and Centre for Danish Studies, the University of Lund (Gothenburg, 2006).

188 Between 1397 and 1593 the Nordic countries were united under one monarch, in the so-called Kalmar Union. However, due to its large geographic size and the differing interests of its national aristocracies, it was to cumbersome to govern and split up into the main kingdoms of Denmark and Sweden, with Norway, Finland and Iceland being secondary parties until well into the modern era.

REYKJAVÍK AND INTERNATIONAL POLITICS

189 "289 US Climate Mayors commit to adopt, honor and uphold Paris Climate Agreement goals", *ClimateMayors* (blog), 6. janúar 2017, https://medium.com/@ClimateMayors/climate-mayors-commit-to-adopt-honor-and-uphold-paris-climate-agreement-goals-ba566e260097.

190 Taiye Selasi, *Don't ask me where I'm from, ask me where I'm local*, Ted Global, 2014, http://www.ted.com/talks/taiye_selasi_don_t_ask_where_i_m_from_ask_where_i_m_a_local.

191 Barber, *If Mayors Ruled the World; Dysfunctional Nations, Rising Cities.*

192 "Pussy Riot gjörningur Jóns Gnarr vekur eftirtekt í Rússlandi", *eyjan.pressan.is*, 8 December 2012, eyjan.is útgáfa, http://eyjan.pressan.is/frettir/2012/08/12/pussy-riot-gjorningur-jons-gnarr-vekur-eftirtekt-i-russlandi/.

193 "Pussy Riot gjörningur Jóns Gnarr vekur eftirtekt í Rússlandi", *eyjan.pressan.is*, 8 December 2012, eyjan.is útgáfa, http://eyjan.pressan.is/frettir/2012/08/12/pussy-riot-gjorningur-jons-gnarr-vekur-eftirtekt-i-russlandi/.

194 "Fundur nr. 5278" (City Council, August 2013), http://reykjavik.is/fundargerd/fundur-nr-5278.

195 "Borgarstjórn 15.9.2015" (Borgarstjórn, 15 September 2015), http://reykjavik.is/fundargerd/borgarstjorn-1592015.

196 "Borgarstjórn 22.9.2015" (Borgarstjórn, 22 September 2015), http://reykjavik.is/fundargerd/borgarstjorn-2292015.

About the Author

Magnus Skjöld (b. 1968, Reykjavik) is an associate professor of politics at Bifröst University, Iceland, who has published on international and regional politics and has been fascinated by societal development for most of his life. In 2018 he spent six months in Kabul, Afghanistan, as a Political Advisor for NATO's Senior Civilian Representative, mainly working on women's rights and gender equality. He has served in the Icelandic Parliament, *Alþingi*, and holds degrees in development economics, politics, philosophy, composition, and European Studies from the University of Cambridge, the University of Iceland, Iceland University of the Arts, and the University of San Francisco. He has four children and two grandchildren and lives in Reykjavík.

You can connect with me on:

- https://mjaldurpublishing.com
- https://www.facebook.com/magnus.skjold.author
- https://www.instagram.com/magnus.skjold.author

Also by Magnus Skjöld

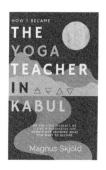

How I Became the Yoga Teacher in Kabul
In this little gem of a book, the author presents his model based on the four elements, earth, air, fire, and water, to help those with multiple interests organise their life and talents so that they manage to flourish and enjoy their efforts in everything they put their mind to. Published in 2023

Climate Ready (with Casey Joy)
Climate-related events are getting worse by the day: storms, heat waves, floods, disruptions and brownouts. "Climate Ready" is a comprehensive guide to prepare for climate change challenges. It covers an introduction to climate science, personal risk assessment, home fortification, sustainable food, energy, emergencies, finances, transportation, community resilience, and health. The book empowers readers to take action and build resilience in the face of climate-related events. Published in 2023.

Made in the USA
Middletown, DE
09 April 2024